Betty Crocker

SNACKS

Betty Crocker

SNACKS

Easy Ways to Satisfy Your Cravings

Houghton Mifflin Harcourt
Boston • New York • 2021

GENERAL MILLS

Global Business Solutions
Director: Heather Polen

Global Business Solutions
Manager: Andrea Kleinschmit

Executive Editor: Cathy
Swanson Wheaton

Recipe Development and
Testing: Betty Crocker Kitchens

Photography: General Mills
Photography Studios

HOUGHTON MIFFLIN HARCOURT

Editorial Director:
Karen Murgolo

Associate Editor: Sarah Kwak

Senior Managing Editor:
Marina Padakis

Production Editor:
Christine Borris

Art Director and Book Design:
Tai Blanche

Senior Production Coordinator:
Kimberly Kiefer

Find more great ideas at
BettyCrocker.com

Published by Houghton Mifflin Harcourt Publishing Company.

For information about permission to reproduce selections from this book, write to Permissions, Houghton Mifflin Harcourt Publishing Company, 3 Park Avenue, New York, New York 10016.

hmhbooks.com

Library of Congress Cataloging-in-Publication Data

Names: Crocker, Betty, author.

Title: Betty Crocker snacks : easy ways to satisfy your cravings / Betty Crocker.

Description: Boston : Houghton Mifflin Harcourt, 2020. | Includes index.

Identifiers: LCCN 2020039116 (print) | LCCN 2020039117 (ebook) | ISBN 9780358363729 (trade paperback) | ISBN 9780358362821 (ebook)

Subjects: LCSH: Snack foods. | Appetizers.

Classification: LCC TX740 .C734 2020 (print) | LCC TX740 (ebook) | DDC 641.5/3—dc23

Find more great ideas at BettyCrocker.com

Manufactured in China

SCP 10 9 8 7 6 5 4 3 2 1

Cover photo, clockwise from top: Frozen Banana Pops (page 266), Spicy Green Bean "Fries" (page 28), Mini Asian Sliders (page 232)

Inspiring America to Cook At Home™

DEAR NIBBLERS,

There are so many delicious reasons to snack! Snacking is perfect if you are eating smaller meals more frequently, rather than three squares; it can be a super strategy for getting more fruits and veggies in your diet; or, when your tummy tank hits empty, snacking will cover you until mealtime.

Maybe you're looking for something to munch while binge-watching your favorite show, or perhaps you want to bring a treat to a party. Whatever the reason, snacks are what we reach for. But all those snack purchases from grocery stores, drive-throughs and gas stations can drain your debit card—fast. Plus, there can be a lot of unwanted ingredients that come along for the ride in pre-packaged snacks.

Making your own snacks can save you money and provide exactly the ingredients you're looking for, such as protein, greens or your favorite indulgence. Or making your own can help you skip the things you're trying to avoid, such as dairy, gluten or high-calorie ingredients. You can choose something to fit your craving, whether it's savory or sweet, spicy, crunchy or even chocolatey and ooey-gooey.

So, let's meet in the kitchen and satisfy those snack cravings right now!

Sincerely,

Betty Crocker

You'll find all these types of recipes inside:

GLUTEN FREE **VEGETARIAN** **VEGAN**

ALL MINE **PARTY READY**

CONTENTS

10 MINUTES OR LESS SAVORY
13
Amazing, Changing Hummus 32

10 MINUTES OR LESS SWEET
51
Make Your Own Oat "Milk" 72

20 MINUTES OR LESS SAVORY
105
Roasted Beans 3 Ways 146

20 MINUTES OR LESS SWEET
185
Energy Balls 3 Ways 204

30 MINUTES OR LESS SAVORY
225
Potato Nugget Hacks 236

30 MINUTES OR LESS SWEET
255
Frozen Banana Pops 266

INDEX
281

SNACKING

WHAT'S YOUR SNACKING PLEASURE?

Looking for super-quick, savory or sweet snacks? The recipes in this book are divided by the prep time it takes to make them—10, 20 or 30 minutes or less—as well as further divided by sweet or savory. If you're craving a hearty savory snack—check out the **20 Minutes or Less Savory Snacks**. Looking for something to bring to a party? Look for our recipes labeled **Party Ready.** They are big enough to share with a group and sure to bring rave reviews. Want to make a snack just for yourself? Look for **ALL MINE** recipes. They make just one or two servings, so you don't have to share!

A SNACK FOR EVERY CRAVING

From spur-of-the moment **Cheddar Cauliflower "Popcorn"** (page 27) to a gluten-free **Iced Oat "Milk" Chai Latte** (page 74) that's whipped up in minutes, and tummy-filling **Kimchi-Chicken Quesadillas** (page 112) to decadent **Coconut-Chocolate–Covered Cheesecake Bites** (page 274), we've got recipes to satisfy those cravings and reasons to nosh. Check out this snack-size sampling (right) of recipes you'll find inside this book.

GLUTEN–FREE, VEGETARIAN AND VEGAN COOKING

WHAT IS GLUTEN?

Whether you have a gluten sensitivity or you just choose to avoid things with gluten, here's what you need to know to cook or bake gluten free. Gluten is a protein that naturally occurs in certain grains like wheat, barley, rye and some oats. But foods that are naturally gluten free can contain gluten if they have been processed in a plant with foods that contain gluten or were made in a kitchen with utensils that have been used with gluten-containing foods. That's where it can get a little tricky.

GLUTEN FREE

Chocolate, Strawberry
and Oat "Milk" Shakes

Herbed Goat Cheese
Pizza Poppers

Slow-Cooker Bourbon-
Honey BBQ Wings

No-Bake Puffed
Quinoa and Fruit Bars

HIGH FIBER

Chick Pea and
Veggie Burgers

Spinach-Feta
Naan Pizzas

Roasted Beans
3 Ways

ALL MINE

Bacon Mac and
Cheese Bowl

Greek-Style Cottage
Cheese Snack Bowl

Cookie Butter
Mug Cakes

Blueberry
Crunch Parfait

CHOCOLATE
INDULGENCES

Chocolate-Coconut
Marshmallow Dip

Raspberry Cream-
Filled Chocolates

Chocolate–Peanut
Butter Snack Mix

IS IT GLUTEN FREE?

In the gluten-free recipes in this book, we've specifically called for gluten-free ingredients where they aren't naturally gluten free. Many products will say "gluten free" somewhere on the label, but many do not—and you can't be sure if they contain any gluten. **Always read labels to make sure each recipe ingredient is gluten free. Products and ingredient sources can change.** If you're unsure if it's gluten free—call the manufacturer.

COMMON INGREDIENTS THAT CAN CONTAIN GLUTEN

Barbecue sauces and marinades	Miso
Broth or gravies	Rotisserie chicken
Candy	Processed meats
Coating mixes	Salad dressings
Flavorings	Sauces
Imitation bacon	Soy sauce
Meat substitutes	Soups

GLUTEN-FREE TIPS

KEEP SEPARATE For those who are gluten sensitive, keeping things separate matters. It's necessary to keep a dedicated space for storing ingredients for cooking gluten free, as well as a separate space for storing cutting boards and utensils such as rubber scrapers and metal spatulas. Because it's hard to completely remove any gluten residue from these kitchen items, gluten-free foods can easily become contaminated with gluten with even the tiniest bit left on a utensil or countertop—and that can have a detrimental effect on those who are sensitive to gluten.

PAN PREP Grease pans with solid shortening or use cooking spray that doesn't contain flour.

LIQUID ABSORPTION Gluten-free doughs may absorb liquids differently than wheat dough, so be sure to follow directions carefully.

DOUGH HANDLING Gluten-free doughs tend to be sticky. Wet or grease hands to prevent the dough from sticking.

IS IT DONE YET? Gluten-free baked goods often look done before they actually are, so follow the doneness directions given, in addition to bake time.

VEGETARIAN AND VEGAN

There are several types of vegetarian diets, ranging from the least-strict food choices (occasionally eating fish and seafood, poultry or meat) to the strictest food choices (omitting dairy products and all fish, seafood, poultry and meat). A vegan diet follows the strictest vegetarian diet while also omitting eggs and any product made from an ingredient that is animal based.

UNDERSTANDING INGREDIENT CHOICES

Look for vegetarian and vegan recipes through this book. We call specifically for vegan or organic ingredients where necessary, as some may use an animal-based ingredient in processing: Dairy-based ingredients such as yogurt, sour cream and pudding may contain gelatin, and some Parmesan cheese is made with animal rennet, which wouldn't be vegan. Recipes labeled vegan in this book are also, by default, vegetarian.

Always read labels to make sure each recipe ingredient is vegan or vegetarian. Products and ingredient sources can change.

10 MINUTES OR LESS

SAVORY

JALAPEÑO-EVERYTHING-SEASONED PARMESAN CRISPS

PREP TIME: 10 Minutes • **START TO FINISH:** 25 Minutes • **MAKES:** 12 crisps

¾ cup (3 oz) shredded Parmesan cheese (12 tablespoons)
1 teaspoon sesame seed
1 teaspoon poppy seed
½ teaspoon garlic powder
½ teaspoon dried minced onion
1 medium jalapeño chile or mini bell pepper, thinly sliced

1 Heat oven to 350°F. Spray large cookie sheet with cooking spray.

2 Spoon level tablespoons of cheese into 12 mounds on pan. Spread each mound into 3-inch circle.

3 In small bowl, stir remaining ingredients except jalapeño. Sprinkle about ¼ teaspoon seed mixture evenly over each cheese circle. Top with jalapeño.

4 Bake 8 to 10 minutes or until golden brown and crisp. Cool on cookie sheet 1 minute; carefully remove from pan and cool on cooling rack at least 5 minutes.

1 Crisp: Calories 30; Total Fat 2g (Saturated Fat 1g, Trans Fat 0g); Cholesterol 0mg; Sodium 85mg; Total Carbohydrate 0g (Dietary Fiber 0g); Protein 2g **Exchanges:** ½ Lean Meat **Carbohydrate Choices:** 0

CHANGE IT UP: Look for red and green jalapeño chiles and use a combination of both for a colorful presentation. If you don't like heat, use mini bell peppers instead.

KITCHEN SECRET: Wear gloves when cutting chiles, as the oils can burn your skin and your eyes, if you touch your hands to your eyes.

KITCHEN SECRET: Not only are these a yummy snack, but they also make a delightful accompaniment to your favorite soup or salad. Or you can make them a few hours ahead to serve as a delicious cocktail party appetizer.

KITCHEN SECRET: These crisps need to cool at least 5 minutes to allow the cheese to firm up, for easy pickup without crumbling.

COOKING GLUTEN FREE? Always read labels to make sure *each* recipe ingredient is gluten free. Products and ingredient sources can change.

SALSA-AVOCADO CHEESE SNACKS

PREP TIME: 10 Minutes • **START TO FINISH:** 10 Minutes • **MAKES:** 2 servings (3 tortilla chips each)

6 round tortilla chips (from 13-oz bag) or other large tortilla chips

6 (¼-inch-thick) slices extra-sharp cheddar cheese (from 8-oz package)

2 tablespoons salsa

2 (¼-inch-thick) slices avocado, cut into thirds

Fresh cilantro leaves

1 Arrange tortilla chips in a single layer on a microwavable plate. Top each chip with 1 cheese slice; microwave uncovered on High 10 to 20 seconds or until cheese melts.

2 Top with remaining ingredients. Serve immediately.

1 Serving: Calories 180 (Calories from Fat 110); Total Fat 12g (Saturated Fat 6g, Trans Fat 0g); Cholesterol 25mg; Sodium 320mg; Total Carbohydrate 9g (Dietary Fiber 1g, Sugars 0g); Protein 7g **Exchanges:** ½ Other Carbohydrate, 1 High-Fat Meat, 1 Fat **Carbohydrate Choices:** ½

CHANGE IT UP: Raid your fridge! Salsa verde or Buffalo wing sauce can be used in place of salsa. Pepper Jack, Monterey Jack, Colby–Monterey Jack or even American cheese would also be fabulous. Add a bit more protein with cooked shrimp, thinly sliced cooked chicken breast or cooked bacon—yum!

COOKING GLUTEN FREE? Always read labels to make sure *each* recipe ingredient is gluten free. Products and ingredient sources can change.

SAVORY CAPRESE BOWL

PREP TIME: 10 Minutes • **START TO FINISH:** 10 Minutes • **MAKES:** 1 serving

1²/₃ cups plain yogurt

¼ cup quartered cherry tomatoes

½ teaspoon balsamic vinegar

⅛ teaspoon fine sea salt

⅛ teaspoon pepper

1 tablespoon thinly sliced fresh basil leaves

½ teaspoon olive oil

1 tablespoon pine nuts, toasted

1 Spoon yogurt into shallow bowl.

2 In small bowl, mix tomatoes, vinegar, salt and pepper. Top yogurt with tomato mixture and basil. Drizzle with olive oil; top with pine nuts. Serve immediately.

1 Serving: Calories 350; Total Fat 14g (Saturated Fat 5g, Trans Fat 0g); Cholesterol 25mg; Sodium 590mg; Total Carbohydrate 33g (Dietary Fiber 1g); Protein 23g **Exchanges:** ½ Starch, 2 Low-Fat Milk, ½ Vegetable, ½ Very Lean Meat, ½ Fat **Carbohydrate Choices:** 2

KITCHEN SECRET: An easy way to slice basil is to stack the leaves, aligning the stems. Roll the leaves together like a cigar and thinly slice crosswise.

KITCHEN SECRET: To toast pine nuts, put them in 8-inch nonstick skillet over medium-high heat. Toast 2 to 3 minutes, stirring constantly, until lightly golden. Remove from the skillet and cool until ready to use.

COOKING GLUTEN FREE? Always read labels to make sure *each* ingredient is gluten free. Products and ingredient sources can change.

GREEK-STYLE COTTAGE CHEESE SNACK BOWL

PREP TIME: 10 Minutes • **START TO FINISH:** 10 Minutes • **MAKES:** 1 serving

⅔ cup cottage cheese

½ teaspoon gluten-free Greek seasoning

¼ cup chick peas or garbanzo beans (from 15-oz can), drained, rinsed

2 tablespoons chopped tomato

2 tablespoons chopped cucumber

2 teaspoons chopped fresh parsley

In individual serving bowl, stir together cottage cheese and Greek seasoning. Top with chick peas, tomato and cucumber. Sprinkle with parsley.

1 Serving: Calories 190; Total Fat 4.5g (Saturated Fat 2g, Trans Fat 0g); Cholesterol 20mg; Sodium 1050mg; Total Carbohydrate 18g (Dietary Fiber 3g); Protein 19g **Exchanges:** ½ Starch, ½ Other Carbohydrate, 2½ Very Lean Meat, ½ Fat **Carbohydrate Choices:** 1

KITCHEN SECRET: No Greek seasoning on hand? You can use ¼ teaspoon each dried oregano leaves, dried thyme leaves and dried basil leaves and a dash salt.

CHANGE IT UP: Serve this easy snack bowl with gluten-free pita chips or use mini bell peppers, cut in half and seeded, as dippers. Prepare everything ahead of time for a grab-and-go lunch option.

COOKING GLUTEN FREE? Always read labels to make sure *each* recipe ingredient is gluten free. Products and ingredient sources can change.

BACON MAC AND CHEESE BOWL

PREP TIME: 10 Minutes • **START TO FINISH:** 10 Minutes • **MAKES:** 1 serving (1½ cups)

¾ cup water

1 cup uncooked rotini pasta (from 16-oz box)

1 cup shredded American cheese (4 oz)

2 slices bacon, crisply cooked, crumbled

¼ cup shredded Parmesan cheese (1 oz)

2 tablespoons milk

⅛ teaspoon pepper

1 In shallow 2½-cup microwavable serving bowl, microwave water uncovered on High 1 minute. Stir in pasta; cover with waxed paper. Microwave on High 7 to 8 minutes, stirring every 2 minutes, until pasta is tender. If necessary, add 1 to 2 tablespoons water and microwave an additional minute until pasta is tender.

2 Set aside 1 tablespoon of the American cheese and 1 tablespoon of the bacon. Stir remaining American cheese, bacon and the other ingredients into pasta. Microwave uncovered on High 40 to 60 seconds, stirring after about 25 seconds, until cheese is melted. Top with reserved bacon and American cheese; serve.

1 Serving: Calories 1170; Total Fat 51g (Saturated Fat 28g, Trans Fat 1.5g); Cholesterol 150mg; Sodium 2980mg; Total Carbohydrate 118g (Dietary Fiber 6g); Protein 57g **Exchanges:** 7 Starch, 1 Other Carbohydrate, 1 Lean Meat, 4 High-Fat Meat, 2½ Fat **Carbohydrate Choices:** 8

KITCHEN SECRET: You can find shredded American cheese in some larger grocery stores. If it's not available, shred American cheese—not American cheese product, which will be too soft and difficult to shred. If the cheese you have is too soft to shred, place it in the freezer for 30 minutes.

KITCHEN SECRET: For the success of this recipe, use a shallow 2½-cup serving bowl. If the bowl is not large enough, the water can boil over the side and the pasta won't get tender.

CHANGE IT UP: Top your mac and cheese with chopped green onion for a bit of green, if you like.

MEDITERRANEAN WATERMELON "FRIES" WITH CREAMY FETA DIP

PREP TIME: 10 Minutes • **START TO FINISH:** 10 Minutes • **MAKES:** 5 servings (1 cup watermelon "fries" and ¼ cup dip each)

CREAMY FETA DIP

- ¼ cup crumbled feta cheese (1 oz)
- 1 container (6 to 7 oz) plain Greek yogurt
- ⅓ cup finely chopped cucumber
- 2 tablespoons milk
- 1 tablespoon chopped fresh mint leaves

WATERMELON "FRIES"

- 5 cups (3×½×½-inch) seedless watermelon strips (about ¼ small melon)
- ½ teaspoon dried oregano leaves
- ¼ teaspoon salt
- ¼ teaspoon garlic powder
- ¼ teaspoon coarse ground black pepper

1. In small bowl, mash cheese with fork to break up large crumbles. Stir in remaining Creamy Feta Dip ingredients. Cover and refrigerate until ready to serve.

2. Arrange watermelon strips on serving platter.

3. In small bowl, stir together oregano, salt, garlic powder and pepper. Sprinkle oregano mixture evenly over watermelon. Serve with Creamy Feta Dip.

1 Serving: Calories 100; Total Fat 2.5g (Saturated Fat 1.5g, Trans Fat 0g); Cholesterol 10mg; Sodium 200mg; Total Carbohydrate 14g (Dietary Fiber 0g); Protein 5g **Exchanges:** 1 Fruit, ½ Low-Fat Milk **Carbohydrate Choices:** 1

KITCHEN SECRET: Selecting a flavorful, ripe watermelon can be hit or miss. For the best chance of getting the tastiest melon, pick up the melon. It should feel heavy for its size. There should be a pale-yellow area where it sat on the field to ripen.

KITCHEN SECRET: The Creamy Feta Dip and herb mixture can be made ahead. If you want to garnish the dip, sprinkle it with additional mint just before serving. Arrange the watermelon on the platter, cover and refrigerate up to 2 hours ahead. But sprinkle the herb mixture on the watermelon just before serving to keep the watermelon from becoming watery.

COOKING GLUTEN FREE? Always read labels to make sure *each* recipe ingredient is gluten free. Products and ingredient sources can change.

CHEDDAR CAULIFLOWER "POPCORN"

PREP TIME: 10 Minutes　•　**START TO FINISH:** 35 Minutes　•　**MAKES:** 3 servings (½ cup each)

3 cups small cauliflower florets
1 tablespoon olive oil
¼ teaspoon salt
⅛ teaspoon pepper
⅓ cup finely shredded
　sharp cheddar cheese
　(a little under 3 oz)

1 Heat oven to 450°F.

2 In large bowl, toss cauliflower, oil, salt and pepper until well mixed. Spread mixture on ungreased 15×10×1-inch pan.

3 Bake 18 to 22 minutes, stirring after about 10 minutes, until light golden brown and crisp-tender. Sprinkle with cheese. Let stand about 1 minute or until cheese is melted.

1 Serving: Calories 120; Total Fat 9g (Saturated Fat 3g, Trans Fat 0g); Cholesterol 10mg; Sodium 310mg; Total Carbohydrate 6g (Dietary Fiber 2g); Protein 5g **Exchanges:** 1 Vegetable, ½ High-Fat Meat, 1 Fat **Carbohydrate Choices:** ½

KITCHEN SECRET: Serve this tasty cauliflower "popcorn" in fun cooking parchment–lined paper restaurant trays.

CHANGE IT UP: Try spicing things up by adding ⅛ teaspoon ground red pepper (cayenne).

COOKING GLUTEN FREE? Always read labels to make sure *each* recipe ingredient is gluten free. Products and ingredient sources can change.

SPICY GREEN BEAN "FRIES"

PREP TIME: 10 Minutes • **START TO FINISH:** 25 Minutes • **MAKES:** 4 servings

1 tablespoon all-purpose flour

1½ lb fresh green beans, trimmed

2 eggs

2 tablespoons Thai chili paste (from 6.5-oz jar)

¾ cup plain panko crispy bread crumbs

3 tablespoons grated Parmesan cheese

½ teaspoon salt

Cooking spray

1 Heat oven to 425°F. Spray bottom of 15x10-inch pan with sides with cooking spray.

2 In 1-gallon resealable food-storage plastic bag, place flour. Add beans and seal bag; shake until well coated.

3 In shallow bowl, beat eggs and chili paste until well mixed. In another shallow bowl, mix bread crumbs, cheese and salt.

4 Working in batches of 6 or 7 beans at a time, dip beans in egg mixture; roll in bread crumb mixture to coat. Place beans in single layer in baking pan. Lightly spray beans with cooking spray.

5 Bake 10 to 14 minutes or until crisp and golden brown.

1 Serving: Calories 210; Total Fat 5g (Saturated Fat 1.5g, Trans Fat 0g); Cholesterol 95mg; Sodium 660mg; Total Carbohydrate 30g (Dietary Fiber 4g); Protein 10g **Exchanges:** 1 Starch, 3 Vegetable, 1 Fat **Carbohydrate Choices:** 2

KITCHEN SECRET: Thai chili paste is a blend of red chiles and Thai spices. It can be found in the Asian aisle of your favorite grocery store.

CHANGE IT UP: These crispy beans would be delicious with many of your favorite sauces or salad dressings. Try teriyaki, peanut or orange-ginger sauce, or poppy seed, sesame-ginger or chipotle ranch dressing.

Clockwise from top: Chipotle Ranch Dressing, Orange-Ginger Sauce, Teriyaki Sauce

ITALIAN CARROT "FRIES"

PREP TIME: 10 Minutes • **START TO FINISH:** 30 Minutes • **MAKES:** 4 servings (9 "fries" each)

3 medium carrots, peeled

2 tablespoons grated Parmesan cheese

2 teaspoons all-purpose flour

1½ teaspoons Italian salad dressing mix (from 0.6-oz package)

1 Heat oven to 425°F. Line cookie sheet with heavy-duty foil; spray with cooking spray.

2 Cut carrots crosswise into about 3-inch lengths. Cut each piece in half lengthwise; cut pieces lengthwise again into thirds to make fry-size sticks.

3 In 1-gallon resealable food-storage plastic bag, blend cheese, flour and dry salad dressing mix. Add carrots and seal bag; toss to coat. Spread carrots in single layer on cookie sheet. Sprinkle remaining cheese mixture from bag over carrots.

4 Bake for 10 minutes. Turn carrots; bake an additional 7 to 10 minutes or until edges are browned and begin to crisp. Serve immediately.

1 Serving: Calories 40; Total Fat 1g (Saturated Fat 0.5g, Trans Fat 0g); Cholesterol 0mg; Sodium 170mg; Total Carbohydrate 6g (Dietary Fiber 1g); Protein 1g **Exchanges:** 1 Vegetable **Carbohydrate Choices:** ½

KITCHEN SECRET: To garnish, arrange on a serving plate and sprinkle with chopped parsley and additional grated Parmesan cheese.

CHANGE IT UP: These delicious "fries" are seasoned so well they can stand on their own—nothing else required. But if you love to dip, try them with French onion dip, aioli, hummus or seasoned sour cream. Either way, you will become a fan!

AMAZING, CHANGING HUMMUS

It's almost embarrassingly easy. Making your own fresh hummus takes just a few ingredients and a whirl in your food processor. It's a guilt-free, delicious way to satisfy the "hangries."

The fresh flavor—and ease on your wallet—of homemade hummus will win every time over the store-bought stuff. And really, you can whip it up just about as fast as you can open the ready-made variety, so why not make your own? Tickle your taste buds by changing it up with one of these simple swaps or additions for a different snack each time:

HUMMUS FLAVORS

BROCCOLI Add 1 cup cooked and cooled broccoli florets to the blender.

TZATZIKI TWIST Swirl a tablespoon or two of prepared tzatziki sauce into prepared hummus just before serving. Top hummus with chopped cucumber and tomato, drizzle with olive oil and sprinkle with herbs.

SPICY SWEET PEA Add 1 cup cooked and cooled frozen sweet peas and 2 teaspoons prepared horseradish to the blender. Top with additional cooked peas.

ROASTED RED PEPPER Omit cumin and add ⅓ cup drained roasted red bell peppers to the blender. Top with jalapeño slices and cilantro leaves.

SWEET POTATO Increase salt to 1½ teaspoons and cumin to 1 teaspoon. Add 1 large cooked, cooled and peeled dark orange sweet potato, 3 tablespoons olive oil and 2 teaspoons smoked paprika to the blender. Top with roasted salted hulled pumpkin seeds (pepitas) and a dash more paprika.

TACO Omit cumin. Add 1 tablespoon taco seasoning mix to the blender. Top with crushed red pepper flakes and jalapeño chile slices.

WHITE BEAN Substitute 1 (15.5-oz) can drained great northern beans (reserve 2 tablespoons of the liquid) for the chick peas. Increase garlic to 2 cloves. Add the reserved bean liquid and 2 teaspoons olive oil to the blender.

Spicy Sweet Pea

Roasted Red Pepper

Easy Hummus
(recipe on page 34)

White Bean

Sweet Potato

33

GLUTEN FREE **VEGETARIAN** **VEGAN** **PARTY READY**

EASY HUMMUS

PREP TIME: 5 Minutes • **START TO FINISH:** 5 Minutes • **MAKES:** 12 servings (2 tablespoons each)

1 can (15 oz) chick peas or garbanzo beans, drained, ¼ cup liquid reserved

3 tablespoons fresh lemon juice

¼ cup sesame tahini paste

1 clove garlic, peeled

1 teaspoon salt

¼ teaspoon ground cumin

In blender, place all ingredients, including reserved bean liquid. Cover; blend about 1 minute or until mixture is smooth.

1 Serving: Calories 70 (Calories from Fat 30); Total Fat 3.5g (Saturated Fat 0g, Trans Fat 0g); Cholesterol 0mg; Sodium 250mg; Total Carbohydrate 7g (Dietary Fiber 2g, Sugars 1g); Protein 2g **Exchanges:** ½ Starch, ½ Fat **Carbohydrate Choices:** ½

KITCHEN SECRET: Sesame tahini paste is a Middle Eastern and eastern Mediterranean condiment made from sesame seed. It's a staple in hummus and can also stand on its own as a dip for veggies or a sandwich spread.

KITCHEN SECRET: Serve hummus with a vegan version of pita bread or crackers, chips, naan, French bread slices or your favorite veggie dippers.

COOKING GLUTEN FREE OR VEGAN? Always read labels to make sure *each* recipe ingredient is gluten free or vegan. Products and ingredient sources can change.

HOW TO STORE: Store covered in the refrigerator up to 5 days.

HUMMUS OLIVE SPREAD

PREP TIME: 10 Minutes • **START TO FINISH:** 10 Minutes • **MAKES:** 10 servings (2 tablespoons spread and 4 pita wedges each)

1 container (7 oz) plain hummus

½ cup pitted Kalamata and/or Spanish olives, chopped, or 1 can (4 ¼ oz) chopped ripe olives, drained

1 tablespoon Greek vinaigrette or zesty gluten-free fat-free Italian dressing

7 gluten-free pita breads (6 inches in diameter), each cut into 6 wedges

1️⃣ Spread hummus on 8- to 10-inch serving plate.

2️⃣ Mix olives and vinaigrette in small bowl. Spoon over hummus. Serve with pita bread wedges.

1 Serving: Calories 160; Total Fat 3.5g (Saturated Fat 0.5g, Trans Fat 0g); Cholesterol 0mg; Sodium 370mg; Total Carbohydrate 27g (Dietary Fiber 2g); Protein 5g **Exchanges:** ½ Starch, 1½ Other Carbohydrate, ½ Very Lean Meat, ½ Fat **Carbohydrate Choices:** 2

COOKING GLUTEN FREE OR VEGAN? Always read labels to make sure *each* recipe ingredient is gluten free or vegan. Products and ingredient sources can change.

SUN-DRIED TOMATO AND FETA SPREAD

PREP TIME: 10 Minutes • **START TO FINISH:** 10 Minutes • **MAKES:** 12 servings (2 tablespoons each)

¾ cup plain Greek yogurt

½ cup crumbled feta cheese (2 oz)

⅓ cup sun-dried tomatoes in oil, drained, 1 tablespoon oil reserved

⅛ teaspoon pepper

2 tablespoons coarsely chopped fresh basil leaves

Fresh broccoli or cauliflower florets, carrot or jicama sticks, if desired

In food processor, place yogurt, cheese, tomatoes, reserved oil and pepper. Cover; process until well mixed but not pureed. Add basil; pulse to mix through. Serve with fresh veggies.

1 Serving: Calories 40; Total Fat 3g (Saturated Fat 1g, Trans Fat 0g); Cholesterol 5mg; Sodium 65mg; Total Carbohydrate 2g (Dietary Fiber 0g); Protein 2g **Exchanges:** ½ Very Lean Meat, ½ Fat **Carbohydrate Choices:** 0

KITCHEN SECRET: Sun-dried tomatoes are available dry or packed in oil. The oil-packed variety is best for this recipe because they are softer and blend into the spread more easily.

CHANGE IT UP: Stir in some chopped pitted kalamata olives after processing for a color and flavor boost.

KITCHEN SECRET: Another great way to enjoy this dip is to serve it with your favorite gluten-free crackers or gluten-free bread. Flavored gluten-free crackers would add another layer of flavor!

COOKING GLUTEN FREE? Always read labels to make sure *each* recipe ingredient is gluten free. Products and ingredient sources can change.

FIRE-ROASTED TOMATO HUMMUS

PREP TIME: 10 Minutes • **START TO FINISH:** 10 Minutes • **MAKES:** 16 servings (2 tablespoons hummus and 2 pita wedges each)

1 can (14.5 oz) fire-roasted diced tomatoes, well drained

1 can (15 oz) chick peas or garbanzo beans, drained, rinsed

2 tablespoons olive oil

1 tablespoon sesame tahini paste

1 clove garlic, finely chopped

2 teaspoons fresh lemon juice

½ teaspoon salt

⅛ teaspoon crushed red pepper flakes

4 pita (pocket) breads, each cut into 8 wedges

① Reserve 2 tablespoons of the tomatoes for garnish. In food processor, put remaining tomatoes and all remaining ingredients except pita bread. Cover; process about 1 minute or until smooth.

② Spoon hummus into shallow serving dish; spoon reserved tomatoes in small mound in center. Serve with pita wedges.

1 Serving: Calories 90; Total Fat 3g (Saturated Fat 0g, Trans Fat 0g); Cholesterol 0mg; Sodium 220mg; Total Carbohydrate 13g (Dietary Fiber 2g); Protein 3g **Exchanges:** 1 Starch, ½ Fat **Carbohydrate Choices:** 1

CHANGE IT UP: Serve with cut-up fresh vegetables, pita chips or crackers instead of pita bread.

CHANGE IT UP: Love basil? Add ¼ cup chopped fresh basil leaves to the prepared hummus and process 15 to 30 seconds longer.

CHANGE IT UP: For Cilantro–Green Chile Hummus: Increase pepper flakes to ¼ teaspoon and add ¼ cup chopped fresh cilantro, 3 tablespoons canned chopped green chiles and ¼ teaspoon ground cumin. Process 15 to 30 seconds longer.

COOKING VEGAN? Always read labels to make sure *each* recipe ingredient is vegan. Products and ingredient sources can change.

SOUTHWEST TACO DIP

PREP TIME: 10 Minutes   •   **START TO FINISH:** 10 Minutes   •   **MAKES:** 8 servings (2 tablespoons each)

2 cups plain fat-free yogurt

¼ cup reduced-fat mayonnaise or salad dressing

2 teaspoons chili powder

1 teaspoon onion powder

½ teaspoon ground cumin

¼ teaspoon salt

¼ cup chopped fresh cilantro

2 tablespoons chopped green onions (2 medium)

2 tablespoons chopped tomato

In medium bowl, mix first 8 ingredients. Top with chopped tomato.

1 Serving: Calories 60; Total Fat 2.5g (Saturated Fat 0g, Trans Fat 0g); Cholesterol 0mg; Sodium 180mg; Total Carbohydrate 6g (Dietary Fiber 0g); Protein 3g **Exchanges:** ½ Skim Milk, ½ Fat **Carbohydrate Choices:** ½

KITCHEN SECRET: Get your gathering off to a great start with this low-fat dip. Tortilla chips and fresh veggies such as baby carrots, sugar snap peas, or grape tomatoes all make great dippers.

KITCHEN SECRET: You can make the dip up to a day ahead, cover and refrigerate. Top with tomato just before serving.

COOKING GLUTEN FREE? Always read labels to make sure *each* recipe ingredient is gluten free. Products and ingredient sources can change.

BUFFALO CHICKEN DIP

PREP TIME: 10 Minutes • **START TO FINISH:** 15 Minutes • **MAKES:** 16 servings (2 tablespoons each)

1 can (10 oz) chunk chicken, drained, chopped

1 package (8 oz) cream cheese, softened

½ cup gluten-free chunky blue cheese dressing

1 to 2 tablespoons gluten-free Buffalo wing sauce

1 medium stalk celery, finely chopped (½ cup)

1 In medium microwavable bowl, mix chicken, cream cheese, dressing and wing sauce. Cover and microwave on High 2 to 3 minutes or until hot.

2 Stir in celery. Spoon into serving dish.

1 Serving: Calories 80; Total Fat 6g (Saturated Fat 4g, Trans Fat 0g); Cholesterol 25mg; Sodium 160mg; Total Carbohydrate 1g (Dietary Fiber 0g); Protein 4g **Exchanges:** ½ Very Lean Meat, 1 Fat **Carbohydrate Choices:** 0

CHANGE IT UP: Got leftover dip? Use it as a sandwich filling! Spread leftover dip on a gluten-free bun and add a leaf of lettuce and sliced tomato and onion.

KITCHEN SECRET: If you like, top this dip with crumbled blue cheese and a celery leaf; serve with gluten-free pita chips.

COOKING GLUTEN FREE? Always read labels to make sure *each* recipe ingredient is gluten free. Products and ingredient sources can change.

SPICY ROASTED NUT TRAIL MIX

PREP TIME: 10 Minutes   •   **START TO FINISH:** 20 Minutes   •   **MAKES:** 4 servings (½ cup each)

GLAZE

- 2 tablespoons pure maple syrup or maple-flavored syrup
- ½ teaspoon ground coriander
- ½ teaspoon garlic powder
- ¼ teaspoon ground red pepper (cayenne)
- 1 tablespoon butter

TRAIL MIX

- 1 cup salted mixed nuts
- ½ cup gluten-free pretzels
- ¼ cup sweetened dried cranberries
- ¼ cup roasted salted hulled pumpkin seeds (pepitas)
- 1 tablespoon chopped fresh cilantro

1 In medium microwavable bowl, stir together all Glaze ingredients. Microwave uncovered on High 30 to 40 seconds or until bubbly and mixture can be stirred until butter is almost melted.

2 Stir in all Trail Mix ingredients except cilantro until well coated. Microwave uncovered on High 2 minutes; stir. Microwave about 2 minutes longer or until evenly coated and sticky.

3 Stir in cilantro. Spread on waxed paper; cool about 10 minutes.

1 Serving: Calories 330; Total Fat 23g (Saturated Fat 4g, Trans Fat 0g); Cholesterol 10mg; Sodium 90mg; Total Carbohydrate 24g (Dietary Fiber 3g); Protein 6g **Exchanges:** 1 Starch, ½ Other Carbohydrate, ½ High-Fat Meat, 3½ Fat **Carbohydrate Choices:** 1½

HOW TO STORE: This nutty trail mix can be made ahead. Store in an airtight container at room temperature up to several days. It's the perfect snack for after school, hiking or between running errands on a busy day.

CHANGE IT UP: This recipe uses salted mixed nuts, but you can use salted peanuts or cashews instead, or create your own mixed nuts by mixing and matching your favorites. If you don't need to worry about gluten, try pretzel nuggets for a fun shape that holds the coating deliciously!

COOKING GLUTEN FREE? Always read labels to make sure *each* recipe ingredient is gluten free. Products and ingredient sources can change.

ULTIMATE TAILGATE PARTY MIX

PREP TIME: 10 Minutes • **START TO FINISH:** 10 Minutes • **MAKES:** 24 servings (½ cup each)

6 cups bite-size squares peanut butter oven-toasted rice cereal

3 cups kettle corn

1½ cups football-shaped pretzels or mini pretzel twists

1 cup honey-roasted peanuts

1 cup candy-coated chocolate candies or candy-coated chocolate-covered peanut candies

In large serving bowl, mix all ingredients well.

1 Serving: Calories 140; Total Fat 6g (Saturated Fat 2g, Trans Fat 0g); Cholesterol 0mg; Sodium 125mg; Total Carbohydrate 19g (Dietary Fiber 1g); Protein 3g **Exchanges:** 1 Starch, 1 Fat **Carbohydrate Choices:** 1

CHANGE IT UP: Try different color candy-coated chocolate candies to customize the mix for the season. Or if serving on game day, use your favorite team's colors.

KITCHEN SECRET: This crowd-size recipe can easily be cut in half for your family or a smaller get-together.

BAKED ARTICHOKE AND JALAPEÑO CHEESE SPREAD

PREP TIME: 10 Minutes • **START TO FINISH:** 30 Minutes • **MAKES:** 18 servings (2 tablespoons spread and 4 crackers each)

1 package (8 oz) cream cheese, softened

½ cup mayonnaise or salad dressing

1 jar (6 oz) marinated artichoke hearts, drained, coarsely chopped

¼ cup finely chopped red bell pepper

8 to 10 pickled jalapeño chile slices (from 12-oz jar), drained, chopped

½ cup grated Parmesan cheese

⅓ cup plain panko crispy bread crumbs

72 crackers

1 Heat oven to 400°F. Spray 9-inch glass pie plate with cooking spray.

2 In medium bowl, stir together cream cheese and mayonnaise. Stir in artichokes, bell pepper and jalapeños. Reserve 1 tablespoon of the Parmesan cheese; stir remaining cheese into artichoke mixture.

3 Spread cheese mixture evenly in bottom of pie plate. Sprinkle evenly with bread crumbs and reserved Parmesan cheese.

4 Bake about 20 minutes or just until top is lightly golden. Serve warm with crackers.

1 Serving: Calories 120; Total Fat 10g (Saturated Fat 4g, Trans Fat 0g); Cholesterol 15mg; Sodium 310mg; Total Carbohydrate 3g (Dietary Fiber 0g); Protein 2g **Exchanges:** ½ Medium-Fat Meat, 1½ Fat **Carbohydrate Choices:** 0

CHANGE IT UP: For a dip that's less spicy, use fewer jalapeño slices, or substitute 2 tablespoons chopped green chiles for the jalapeños.

KITCHEN SECRET: Panko bread crumbs are Japanese-style bread crumbs that are bigger and crispier than regular bread crumbs.

KITCHEN SECRET: This delicious dip is addictive! Serve it with water crackers, wheat crackers, baguette slices, fresh veggie dippers or even pizza rolls or potato nuggets.

10 MINUTES OR LESS
SWEET

COCONUT-BERRY "BUBBLE" PARFAIT

PREP TIME: 10 Minutes • **START TO FINISH:** 10 Minutes • **MAKES:** 2 parfaits

2 pouches fruit snacks

2 containers (5.3 oz each) coconut-flavored Greek yogurt

3 tablespoons coconut milk or milk

½ cup sliced fresh strawberries

¼ cup gluten-free fruit-flavored sweetened corn puffs cereal

1. Pour 1 pouch fruit snacks into each of 2 parfait, wine or drinking glasses.

2. In small bowl, mix yogurt and coconut milk. Spoon ¼ cup of the yogurt mixture into each glass. Layer half of the strawberries in each glass. Divide remaining yogurt mixture between glasses. Top each with 2 tablespoons cereal.

1 Parfait: Calories 300; Total Fat 9g (Saturated Fat 7g, Trans Fat 0g); Cholesterol 15mg; Sodium 100mg; Total Carbohydrate 43g (Dietary Fiber 2g); Protein 12g **Exchanges:** ½ Fruit, 1½ Other Carbohydrate, 1 Skim Milk, ½ Very Lean Meat, 1½ Fat **Carbohydrate Choices:** 3

KITCHEN SECRET: We borrowed the bubble idea from the Taiwanese tea-based drink that is served with tapioca pearls in it. The "bubbles" in our yogurt parfaits are fruit snacks that get topped with coconut yogurt, fresh berries and fruity cereal. Adorable to look at and a blast to eat!

CHANGE IT UP: You can customize these parfaits by changing the flavor of yogurt and substituting your favorite cereal.

COOKING GLUTEN FREE? Always read labels to make sure *each* recipe ingredient is gluten free. Products and ingredient sources can change.

DOUBLE CHOCOLATE-DIPPED STRAWBERRY YOGURT CUP

PREP TIME: 5 Minutes • **START TO FINISH:** 5 Minutes • **MAKES:** 1 serving

1 container (6 oz) white chocolate–strawberry or strawberry fat-free yogurt

1 tablespoon diced fresh strawberries

2 teaspoons miniature chocolate chips

Eat about a tablespoon of yogurt out of yogurt container. Stir strawberries and chocolate chips into yogurt with fork until well mixed.

1 Serving: Calories 130; Total Fat 2.5g (Saturated Fat 1.5g, Trans Fat 0g); Cholesterol 0mg; Sodium 80mg; Total Carbohydrate 22g (Dietary Fiber 1g); Protein 6g **Exchanges:** ½ Starch, ½ Other Carbohydrate, ½ Low-Fat Milk **Carbohydrate Choices:** 1½

CHANGE IT UP: It's fun to add whipped cream topping or whipped cream and a drizzle of chocolate sauce on top, or just a few simple chocolate curls for a bit of decadence.

CHANGE IT UP: Like a little crunch? Serve this with gluten-free graham cracker sticks or your favorite gluten-free cookie for dunking.

KITCHEN SECRET: If you want to make this snack to go or serve later, spoon the yogurt into a small food storage container and continue as directed. Cover and refrigerate until serving time.

COOKING GLUTEN FREE? Always read labels to make sure *each* recipe ingredient is gluten free. Products and ingredient sources can change.

BANANA-COCONUT YOGURT CUP

PREP TIME: 5 Minutes • **START TO FINISH:** 5 Minutes • **MAKES:** 1 serving

1 container (6 oz) banana cream pie or very vanilla fat-free yogurt
1 teaspoon sliced almonds
1 teaspoon shredded coconut

Eat about a tablespoon yogurt out of yogurt container. Stir almonds and coconut into yogurt with fork until well distributed.

1 Serving: Calories 110; Total Fat 2g (Saturated Fat 1g, Trans Fat 0g); Cholesterol 0mg; Sodium 85mg; Total Carbohydrate 17g (Dietary Fiber 0g); Protein 6g **Exchanges:** ½ Starch, ½ Low-Fat Milk **Carbohydrate Choices:** 1

CHANGE IT UP: Top with miniature chocolate chips, additional almonds or coconut, or all three, if you like.

CHANGE IT UP: For a tropical taste, use toasted coconut and swap out the almonds for chopped macadamia nuts.

KITCHEN SECRET: If desired, toast almonds and coconut in a dry nonstick skillet 2 to 3 minutes over medium heat, stirring frequently, until almonds and coconut turn light golden brown.

COOKING GLUTEN FREE? Always read labels to make sure *each* recipe ingredient is gluten free. Products and ingredient sources can change.

TURTLE BANANA SPLIT YOGURT CUPS

PREP TIME: 10 Minutes • **START TO FINISH:** 10 Minutes • **MAKES:** 2 banana splits

2 large bananas
1 cup vanilla whole milk yogurt
¼ cup cashew halves and pieces
2 tablespoons caramel topping
1 tablespoon chocolate-flavor syrup
2 teaspoons miniature semisweet chocolate chips

Cut bananas in half lengthwise; place 2 halves in each of 2 small bowls. Top each bowl of bananas with half of the yogurt and cashews. Drizzle with caramel topping and chocolate syrup. Top with chocolate chips. Serve immediately.

1 Banana Split: Calories 440; Total Fat 13g (Saturated Fat 4.5g, Trans Fat 0g); Cholesterol 15mg; Sodium 140mg; Total Carbohydrate 71g (Dietary Fiber 5g); Protein 9g **Exchanges:** 1½ Fruit, 3 Other Carbohydrate, ½ Milk, 1 High-Fat Meat **Carbohydrate Choices:** 5

CHANGE IT UP: For extra fun, serve these turtle sundaes in a gluten-free waffle bowl. Or add chopped, gluten-free chocolate-covered chewy caramels for an extra-indulgent turtle sundae. You could also swap the yogurt with frozen yogurt or ice cream. Add a maraschino cherry on top for a fun garnish!

CHANGE IT UP: Love the sweet-salty thing? Sprinkle the top with a pinch of coarse sea salt.

COOKING GLUTEN FREE? Always read labels to make sure *each* recipe ingredient is gluten free. Products and ingredient sources can change.

FRUITY YOGURT PARFAITS

PREP TIME: 10 Minutes • **START TO FINISH:** 10 Minutes • **MAKES:** 6 servings

3 tubes (2.25 oz each) strawberry yogurt (from 1 lb 2-oz box)

3 tubes (2.25 oz each) strawberry-kiwi yogurt (from 1 lb 2-oz box) or other mixed-fruit flavors

1 cup sliced fresh strawberries

2 medium kiwifruit, peeled, cut into small chunks

In each of 6 small (4- to 6-oz) parfait glasses, alternate layers of each yogurt, sliced strawberries and kiwifruit. Serve or loosely cover and refrigerate up to 3 hours.

1 Serving: Calories 110; Total Fat 2g (Saturated Fat 1g, Trans Fat 0g); Cholesterol 5mg; Sodium 30mg; Total Carbohydrate 19g (Dietary Fiber 1g); Protein 3g **Exchanges:** 1 Fruit, ½ Low-Fat Milk **Carbohydrate Choices:** 1

KITCHEN SECRET: Cut whole strawberries into heart shapes; thread on toothpicks. Garnish each parfait with a strawberry heart. Or top with whipped cream or heart-shaped candy sprinkles.

CHANGE IT UP: Use different combinations of flavored yogurts and fresh fruit to create your own unique parfaits.

PEAR "NACHOS"

PREP TIME: 10 Minutes   •   **START TO FINISH:** 10 Minutes   •   **MAKES:** 4 servings

2 large unpeeled ripe Bartlett pears (about 1 lb)

3 tablespoons caramel topping

¼ teaspoon apple pie spice

2 tablespoons vanilla Greek yogurt

1 tablespoon orange marmalade

3 tablespoons pomegranate seeds or sweetened dried cranberries

2 tablespoons roasted salted hulled pumpkin seeds (pepitas)

2 tablespoons miniature semisweet chocolate chips

1 Cut pears into slices about ¼ inch thick; arrange on platter or serving plate.

2 In small bowl, mix caramel topping and apple pie spice; drizzle over pears.

3 In separate small bowl, mix yogurt and orange marmalade; spoon over pears. Sprinkle with remaining ingredients.

1 Serving: Calories 190; Total Fat 4g (Saturated Fat 1.5g, Trans Fat 0g); Cholesterol 0mg; Sodium 70mg; Total Carbohydrate 36g (Dietary Fiber 4g); Protein 2g **Exchanges:** 1 Starch, ½ Fruit, 1 Other Carbohydrate, ½ Fat **Carbohydrate Choices:** 2½

KITCHEN SECRET: We love Bartlett pears for these fruity "nachos" for their beautifully colored skin and texture. Choose ripe pears, but not overripe, without bruises or soft spots. You can opt for traditional yellow Bartlett pears or use red Bartlett pears for a showy presentation.

CHANGE IT UP: Apples would be just as yummy in place of pears. You could also sprinkle pecans or candied pecans over the nachos along with the other toppings.

COOKING GLUTEN FREE? Always read labels to make sure *each* recipe ingredient is gluten free. Products and ingredient sources can change.

FRUIT FISH

PREP TIME: 5 Minutes   •   **START TO FINISH:** 5 Minutes   •   **MAKES:** 1 serving

2   tablespoons strawberry or blueberry gluten-free cream cheese, softened

1   apple slice, about ½ inch thick

¼   cup assorted fresh fruit

Spread cream cheese on apple slice. Decorate with fruit as desired to look like a fish.

1 Serving: Calories 120; Total Fat 7g (Saturated Fat 4.5g, Trans Fat 0g); Cholesterol 20mg; Sodium 110mg; Total Carbohydrate 12g (Dietary Fiber 1g); Protein 1g **Exchanges:** ½ Fruit, ½ Other Carbohydrate, 1½ Fat **Carbohydrate Choices:** 1

KITCHEN SECRET: There are lots of ways to make different "fish." Some of the fruit you may want to try are strawberry slices, cut grapes, kiwifruit slices, banana slices, orange sections and fresh blueberries or raspberries to create your own special fish.

COOKING GLUTEN FREE? Always read labels to make sure *each* recipe ingredient is gluten free. Products and ingredient sources can change.

STRAWBERRY-LEMON SHORTCAKE BOWL

PREP TIME: 5 Minutes　●　**START TO FINISH:** 5 Minutes　●　**MAKES:** 1 serving

¼ cup vanilla yogurt

¼ cup frozen whipped topping (from 8-oz container), thawed

1 cup fresh strawberries, cut into quarters

¼ cup gluten-free honey-nut O-shaped toasted oat cereal

⅛ teaspoon finely grated lemon zest

1 Into small bowl, spoon yogurt; carefully stir in whipped topping until completely blended.

2 In serving bowl, place strawberries. Top with yogurt mixture, cereal and lemon zest.

1 Serving: Calories 120 (Calories from Fat 70); Total Fat 7g (Saturated Fat 4.5g, Trans Fat 0g); Cholesterol 20mg; Sodium 110mg; Total Carbohydrate 12g (Dietary Fiber 1g, Sugars 9g); Protein 1g **Exchanges:** ½ Fruit, ½ Other Carbohydrate, 1½ Fat **Carbohydrate Choices:** 1

KITCHEN SECRET: Gently stirring in the whipped topping will lighten the texture of the yogurt. Over-stirring will make it runny.

CHANGE IT UP: Use your favorite berries instead in this recipe: raspberries, blackberries or blueberries.

CHANGE IT UP: Got orange or lime on hand? Substitute zest from one of these for the lemon zest. If you like, switch up the flavor of the yogurt to orange or strawberry as well for a big flavor pop!

COOKING GLUTEN FREE? Always read labels to make sure *each* recipe ingredient is gluten free. Products and ingredient sources can change.

CITRUS CRUNCH PARFAIT

PREP TIME: 10 Minutes   •   **START TO FINISH:** 10 Minutes   •   **MAKES:** 1 parfait

½ cup clementine slices, cut in half (1 clementine)

1 container (5.3 oz) vanilla Greek yogurt

½ cup O-shaped oat crunch cinnamon cereal

1 teaspoon honey

In parfait glass or clear drinking glass, layer half of the clementine slices, half of the yogurt and half of the cereal. Repeat layers. Drizzle with honey. Serve immediately.

1 Parfait: Calories 280; Total Fat 2.5g (Saturated Fat 0g, Trans Fat 0g); Cholesterol 0mg; Sodium 170mg; Total Carbohydrate 48g (Dietary Fiber 3g); Protein 17g **Exchanges:** 1 Starch, 1 Fruit, ½ Other Carbohydrate, 1 Skim Milk, 1 Very Lean Meat **Carbohydrate Choices:** 3

CHANGE IT UP: Try substituting orange or grapefruit slices for the clementine slices. Or substitute your favorite berries.

COLD-BREW YOGURT POPS

PREP TIME: 10 Minutes • **START TO FINISH:** 2 Hours 10 Minutes • **MAKES:** 6 pops

¾ cup vanilla Greek yogurt

2 tablespoons chopped dark chocolate candy bar (from 3.1-oz bar)

1 bottle (11 oz) sweetened or unsweetened cold-brew coffee

1 In small bowl, mix yogurt and chocolate. Pour 2 tablespoons of the coffee into each of 6 (3-oz) ice-pop molds; carefully spoon about 2 tablespoons of the yogurt mixture on top of coffee. Repeat with remaining coffee. Cover with mold tops. Freeze pops at least 2 hours or until frozen.

2 To serve, remove pops from molds.

1 Pop: Calories 45; Total Fat 1.5g (Saturated Fat 1g, Trans Fat 0g); Cholesterol 0mg; Sodium 15mg; Total Carbohydrate 5g (Dietary Fiber 0g); Protein 2g **Exchanges:** ½ Other Carbohydrate, ½ Fat **Carbohydrate Choices:** ½

KITCHEN SECRET: To remove the pops from molds, run the sides of the molds under cold water for a few seconds; pops will slide out easily.

KITCHEN SECRET: If you don't have ice-pop molds, you can use 6 (3 oz) paper cups instead. Cover filled cups with foil and insert a craft stick into center of each. Freeze as directed. To serve, peel off paper cups.

COOKING GLUTEN FREE? Always read labels to make sure *each* recipe ingredient is gluten free. Products and ingredient sources can change.

MAKE YOUR OWN OAT "MILK"

Looking for dairy-free alternative "milks" that don't break the bank? You can make your own oat "milk" in 10 minutes with 3 ingredients you probably have in your kitchen!

But don't stop there—use it as the base for the additional super-delicious beverages (starting on page 74) that are also dairy free, gluten free and completely crave-able. We couldn't put these drinks down at the taste panel . . . bet you won't be able to, either!

TIPS FOR MAKING OAT MILK

If you aren't sensitive to gluten, you can use regular old-fashioned oats instead of those that are specifically gluten free, but keep in mind that if you make any of the other drinks from this recipe, then they won't necessarily be gluten free, either.

Iced Oat "Milk" Chai Latte

- We preferred the sweetness and flavor of pure maple syrup over maple-flavored syrup in this recipe. If you like your milk a little sweeter, increase the syrup to 2 tablespoons.

- Don't be tempted to press the oats dry to get all the milk from the wet oats when straining, as it can give the beverage a slimy texture.

- Oat milk can be enjoyed as is (we love it chilled), poured over your morning cereal or as a substitute for milk in pancakes or waffles. Without any other added ingredients, it will thicken if heated, so avoid using it in hot beverages, such as coffee or tea.

- Cover and store the oat milk in the refrigerator up to 3 days. Shake well or stir before using.

Chocolate, Strawberry and Oat "Milk" Shake

Mango-Banana and Oat "Milk" Smoothie

10-Minute Oat "Milk"

10-MINUTE OAT "MILK"

PREP TIME: 10 Minutes   **START TO FINISH:** 10 Minutes   **MAKES:** 4 servings (generous ¾ cup each)

See tips on page 72 for making this versatile beverage.

- 1 cup gluten-free rolled oats
- 4 cups water
- 1 tablespoon pure maple syrup
- ⅛ teaspoon salt

1 In blender, place oats, water, maple syrup and salt. Cover; blend for 20 to 30 seconds on medium speed until well blended. Do not overblend.

2 Line fine-mesh strainer with cheesecloth and place over large bowl. Pour oat mixture into strainer; let drain. Do not press oat mixture to release more liquid. Discard cheesecloth with oat mixture.

3 Transfer oat milk to 1-quart glass jar; cover and refrigerate. Shake well before using.

1 Serving: Calories 90; Total Fat 1.5g (Saturated Fat 0g, Trans Fat 0g); Cholesterol 0mg; Sodium 85mg; Total Carbohydrate 17g (Dietary Fiber 2g); Protein 2g **Exchanges:** 1 Starch **Carbohydrate Choices:** 1

KITCHEN SECRET: Don't be tempted to press the oats dry when straining, as that can result in oat milk with a slimy texture.

KITCHEN SECRET: You can use the oat milk for drinking just as it is or in cold drinks such as smoothies or shakes. Pour it over cereal or use it in pancakes or muffins. Without any added ingredients, it will thicken as it's heated, so avoid using it for hot beverages.

COOKING GLUTEN FREE? Always read labels to make sure *each* recipe ingredient is gluten free. Products and ingredient sources can change.

ICED OAT "MILK" CHAI LATTE

PREP TIME: 5 Minutes   **START TO FINISH:** 10 Minutes   **MAKES:** 1 serving (1½ cups)

- 2 chai tea bags
- ¼ cup boiling water
- 1 cup 10-Minute Oat "Milk"
- 2 teaspoons pure maple syrup
- 1 or 2 dashes ground cinnamon

1 In 2-cup glass measuring cup, steep chai tea bags in boiling water 5 minutes. Remove tea bags; set one aside and discard the other.

2 Add oat milk, maple syrup and 1 dash cinnamon. Open reserved tea bag and add ⅛ teaspoon of the wet tea leaves to oat milk mixture; discard remaining tea and bag. Stir well to blend.

3 Place ice cubes in tall glass. Pour oat milk mixture over ice. Sprinkle with an additional dash cinnamon, if desired. Serve immediately.

1 Serving: Calories 160; Total Fat 2g (Saturated Fat 0g, Trans Fat 0g); Cholesterol 0mg; Sodium 115mg; Total Carbohydrate 32g (Dietary Fiber 3g); Protein 3g **Exchanges:** 1 Starch, 1 Other Carbohydrate, ½ Fat **Carbohydrate Choices:** 2

CHANGE IT UP: For a warm drink, you can put the latte (without ice) in a microwavable cup and microwave just until very warm. But don't overheat it, or the oat milk may thicken. Or make a "Dirty Chai" by adding a shot of espresso!

KITCHEN SECRET: For more sweetness, add additional maple syrup.

COOKING GLUTEN FREE? Use gluten-free oats for the milk. Always read labels to make sure *each* recipe ingredient is gluten free. Products and ingredient sources can change.

CHOCOLATE, STRAWBERRY AND OAT "MILK" SHAKES

PREP TIME: 10 Minutes ● **START TO FINISH:** 10 Minutes ● **MAKES:** 2 servings (about 1⅓ cups each)

- ¾ cup 10-Minute Oat "Milk"
- 1 cup sliced fresh strawberries (6 oz)
- 1 pint gluten-free vanilla nondairy frozen dessert
- 2 tablespoons gluten-free chocolate-flavor syrup

1 In blender, place oat milk and strawberries. Cover; blend about 5 seconds or until smooth.

2 Add frozen dessert. Cover; blend about 15 seconds or just until smooth.

3 Spoon 1 tablespoon of the syrup into bottom of each of 2 tall (12-oz) glasses; tip and rotate glasses to allow syrup to coat bottom and sides of glasses. Fill glasses with shake mixture. Serve immediately.

1 Serving: Calories 380; Total Fat 15g (Saturated Fat 7g, Trans Fat 0g); Cholesterol 0mg; Sodium 150mg; Total Carbohydrate 56g (Dietary Fiber 5g); Protein 5g **Exchanges:** ½ Starch, 1 Fruit, 2 Other Carbohydrate, ½ Skim Milk, 3 Fat **Carbohydrate Choices:** 4

KITCHEN SECRET: Serve these shakes topped with a fresh strawberry and a drizzle of chocolate-flavor syrup. For fun, dress them up with colorful compostable paper drinking straws or long sundae spoons. Or top them with a coarsely crushed gluten-free creme-filled chocolate sandwich cookies for added crunch.

KITCHEN SECRET: Look for a variety of nondairy frozen desserts or dairy-free "ice creams" at many natural food stores and some conventional grocery stores. Coconut milk, almond milk, cashew milk and other ingredients are used as the base in place of dairy cream and/or milk. These desserts all vary in flavor and texture. Any variety would work in this recipe.

COOKING GLUTEN FREE? Always read labels to make sure *each* recipe ingredient is gluten free. Products and ingredient sources can change.

MANGO-BANANA AND OAT "MILK" SMOOTHIES

PREP TIME: 5 Minutes ● **START TO FINISH:** 5 Minutes ● **MAKES:** 3 servings (generous 1 cup each)

- 1¼ cups 10-Minute Oat "Milk," chilled
- 1 bag (10 oz) frozen mango chunks (2 cups)
- 1 medium banana
- 3 whole dates, pitted and coarsely chopped

In blender, place all ingredients. Cover; blend on high speed about 30 seconds or until smooth. Pour into 3 glasses. Serve immediately.

1 Serving: Calories 170; Total Fat 1g (Saturated Fat 0g, Trans Fat 0g); Cholesterol 0mg; Sodium 50mg; Total Carbohydrate 38g (Dietary Fiber 4g); Protein 3g **Exchanges:** 1 Starch, 1½ Fruit **Carbohydrate Choices:** 2½

KITCHEN SECRET: For a slightly sweeter taste increase to 4 dates. For more texture, top with additional banana slices and chopped macadamia nuts.

COOKING GLUTEN FREE? Always read labels to make sure *each* recipe ingredient is gluten free. Products and ingredient sources can change.

RASPBERRY CHOCOLATE HAZELNUT CEREAL "NACHOS"

PREP TIME: 10 Minutes • **START TO FINISH:** 15 Minutes • **MAKES:** 6 servings (about 1½ cups each)

5 cups cinnamon-toast-flavor cereal

3 cups miniature marshmallows

½ cup sliced almonds

⅔ cup hazelnut spread with cocoa

2 cups fresh raspberries

1 Heat oven to 400°F. Line 15×10×1-inch pan with cooking parchment paper.

2 Spread cereal in single layer in pan. Top evenly with marshmallows and almonds. Bake 3 minutes.

3 Place hazelnut spread in small resealable food-storage plastic bag; seal bag. Cut off small corner of bag; squeeze to drizzle half of the hazelnut spread over cereal mixture. Top with raspberries. Drizzle with remaining hazelnut spread. Serve immediately.

1 Serving: Calories 480; Total Fat 17g (Saturated Fat 2g, Trans Fat 0g); Cholesterol 0mg; Sodium 280mg; Total Carbohydrate 75g (Dietary Fiber 6g); Protein 6g **Exchanges:** 1 Starch, 4 Other Carbohydrate, ½ High-Fat Meat, 2½ Fat **Carbohydrate Choices:** 5

CHANGE IT UP: If you don't have raspberries on hand, cut-up fresh strawberries or blueberries are also terrific on these "nachos." Use what you're in the mood for and what you have on hand.

EASY SCRATCH CAKE MIX

PREP TIME: 5 Minutes • **START TO FINISH:** 5 Minutes

TO MAKE 2 CUPS CAKE MIX

- 1⅓ cups all-purpose flour
- ¾ cup sugar
- 1¼ teaspoons baking powder
- ¼ teaspoon salt

TO MAKE 8 CUPS CAKE MIX

- 5⅓ cups all-purpose flour
- 3 cups sugar
- 5 teaspoons baking powder
- 1 teaspoon salt

In medium or large bowl, mix all ingredients for either 2 cups cake mix or 8 cups cake mix until well blended. Use as directed in recipe, or store in tightly covered container in cool, dark location up to 1 month or freeze up to 3 months.

KITCHEN SECRET: Our easy master mix gives you a great head start on dessert! Make 8 cups of the mix so you can store the unused portion and scoop out what you need at a moment's notice.

CONFETTI MUG CAKE

PREP TIME: 5 Minutes • **START TO FINISH:** 15 Minutes • **MAKES:** 1 mug cake

CAKE

- 2 tablespoons butter
- ½ cup Easy Scratch Cake Mix (page 77)
- ¼ cup milk
- ¼ teaspoon vanilla
- ½ teaspoon confetti candy decors or sprinkles

FROSTING

- ¼ cup miniature marshmallows
- ¼ teaspoon confetti candy decors or sprinkles

1 In microwavable mug (10 oz or larger), microwave butter uncovered on High 30 to 45 seconds or until melted. Stir in cake mix, milk and vanilla with fork. Carefully stir in ½ teaspoon confetti until well blended.

2 Microwave uncovered on High 1 to 2 minutes or until toothpick inserted in center comes out clean and cake pulls from sides of mug. (Do not overcook.) Cool 5 minutes.

3 Top cake with marshmallows. Microwave uncovered on High 20 to 30 seconds or until marshmallows are puffed. Immediately sprinkle with ¼ teaspoon candy decors.

1 Serving: Calories 600; Total Fat 25g (Saturated Fat 16g, Trans Fat 1g); Cholesterol 65mg; Sodium 520mg; Total Carbohydrate 85g (Dietary Fiber 1g); Protein 7g **Exchanges:** 2 Starch, 3 ½ Other Carbohydrate, 5 Fat **Carbohydrate Choices:** 5 ½

KITCHEN SECRET: Make sure that the mug holds at least 10 oz liquid, or the cake may overflow.

CHANGE IT UP: Any of your favorite candy sprinkles can be substituted for the confetti candy decors in this cake. Use holiday-themed decors or sprinkles for Easter, Halloween, Christmas or the 4th of July.

COOKIE BUTTER MUG CAKES

PREP TIME: 10 Minutes • **START TO FINISH:** 15 Minutes • **MAKES:** 2 mug cakes

MUG CAKES

- ¾ cup Easy Scratch Cake Mix (page 77)
- ¼ cup milk
- 2 tablespoons cookie butter spread (from 14.1-oz jar)
- ½ teaspoon vanilla
- 1 egg
- ¼ cup chopped gingersnap cookies (about 4 cookies)

TOPPING

- ¾ cup frozen whipped topping (from 8-oz container), thawed
- 1½ tablespoons cookie butter spread (from 14.1-oz jar)

1. Spray 2 microwavable mugs (10 oz or larger) with cooking spray.

2. In medium bowl, mix Mug Cake ingredients except cookies with spoon until well blended. Stir in cookies. Divide batter between mugs.

3. Microwave both mugs uncovered on High 1½ to 2 minutes or until toothpick inserted in center comes out clean. Cool 5 minutes.

4. Meanwhile, in small bowl, mix Topping ingredients with spoon until well blended. Top each cake with Topping.

1 Mug Cake: Calories 570; Total Fat 20g (Saturated Fat 8g, Trans Fat 0g); Cholesterol 95mg; Sodium 410mg; Total Carbohydrate 87g (Dietary Fiber 2g); Protein 10g **Exchanges:** 3 Starch, 3 Other Carbohydrate, 3½ Fat **Carbohydrate Choices:** 6

KITCHEN SECRET: Keep Easy Scratch Cake Mix on hand for quick mug cakes. Confetti Mug Cake (page 79) is another yummy recipe that uses this mix.

KITCHEN SECRET: Top these easy cakes with another cookie for delicious crunch. No gingersnaps on hand? You can omit them or substitute other purchased crisp cookies. Great choices are shortbread, creme-filled chocolate sandwich cookies or fudge-striped shortbread cookies. Love cookie butter? Warm a little in microwave to drizzle over cakes before serving.

SKINNY FLUFFY ORANGE FRUIT DIP

PREP TIME: 10 Minutes • **START TO FINISH:** 10 Minutes • **MAKES:** 12 servings (2 tablespoons each)

- 4 oz (half of 8-oz package) ⅓-less-fat gluten-free cream cheese (Neufchâtel), softened
- 1 container (6 oz) orange crème or French vanilla yogurt
- 2 tablespoons powdered sugar
- 1 tablespoon frozen orange juice concentrate
- ¼ teaspoon vanilla
- ½ cup fat-free frozen whipped topping (from 8-oz container), thawed

1 In medium bowl, beat cream cheese with electric mixer on low speed until smooth.

2 Add yogurt, powdered sugar, orange juice concentrate and vanilla; beat 30 to 60 seconds on low speed until blended and smooth. Gently stir in whipped topping until well blended. Serve immediately or refrigerate covered up to 24 hours.

1 Serving: Calories 50; Total Fat 2.5g (Saturated Fat 1.5g, Trans Fat 0g); Cholesterol 10mg; Sodium 40mg; Total Carbohydrate 5g (Dietary Fiber 0g); Protein 1g **Exchanges:** ½ Starch, ½ Fat **Carbohydrate Choices:** ½

KITCHEN SECRET: Serve this dip with assorted fresh fruits or with gluten-free versions of any of these dippers: angel food cake cubes, low-fat cookies, graham cracker sticks or thin ginger cookies.

COOKING GLUTEN FREE? Always read labels to make sure *each* recipe ingredient is gluten free. Products and ingredient sources can change.

CARAMELIZED BANANA BOWL

PREP TIME: 10 Minutes • **START TO FINISH:** 10 Minutes • **MAKES:** 1 serving

1 ripe small banana, cut into
  ¾-inch slices

1 tablespoon caramel topping

1 container (5.3 oz) vanilla yogurt

1 tablespoon chopped
  roasted almonds

2 tablespoons flaked coconut,
  toasted

① In small microwavable bowl, mix banana and caramel topping. Microwave uncovered on High 30 to 45 seconds, stirring after every 15 seconds, until banana is softened and warmed.

② Spoon yogurt into small bowl. Top with banana mixture, almonds and coconut.

1 Serving: Calories 390; Total Fat 10g (Saturated Fat 5g, Trans Fat 0g); Cholesterol 10mg; Sodium 220mg; Total Carbohydrate 62g (Dietary Fiber 4g); Protein 10g **Exchanges:** 1 Fruit, 2½ Other Carbohydrate, 1 Skim Milk, ½ High-Fat Meat, 1 Fat **Carbohydrate Choices:** 4

CHANGE IT UP: Try topping with cacao nibs or grated chocolate for a bit more decadence!

KITCHEN SECRET: Toasted coconut is delicious for a topping and is great to have on hand. To toast coconut, bake ½ cup flaked coconut uncovered on an ungreased shallow pan in 350°F oven 5 to 7 minutes, stirring occasionally, until golden brown. Toasted coconut may be stored in a resealable food-storage plastic bag at room temperature up to 1 month.

COOKING GLUTEN FREE? Always read labels to make sure *each* recipe ingredient is gluten free. Products and ingredient sources can change.

BLUEBERRY CRUNCH PARFAIT

PREP TIME: 5 Minutes • **START TO FINISH:** 5 Minutes • **MAKES:** 1 parfait

1 container (6 oz) blueberry yogurt
⅓ cup bite-size squares blueberry oven-toasted rice cereal
¼ cup fresh blueberries

In small bowl or parfait dish, layer half each of the yogurt, cereal and blueberries. Repeat layers.

1 Parfait: Calories 220; Total Fat 3g (Saturated Fat 1g, Trans Fat 0g); Cholesterol 10mg; Sodium 170mg; Total Carbohydrate 40g (Dietary Fiber 1g); Protein 6g **Exchanges:** ½ Starch, ½ Fruit, 1½ Other Carbohydrate, ½ Low-Fat Milk **Carbohydrate Choices:** 2½

CHANGE IT UP: Sprinkle with gluten-free granola or a crushed gluten-free granola bar for another crunchy layer of eating enjoyment!

CHANGE IT UP: Love fresh berries? Add sliced strawberries, raspberries or blackberries to the blueberries for mixed berry parfaits.

COOKING GLUTEN FREE? Always read labels to make sure *each* recipe ingredient is gluten free. Products and ingredient sources can change.

CHOCOLATE-COCONUT MARSHMALLOW DIP

PREP TIME: 10 Minutes   •   **START TO FINISH:** 10 Minutes   •   **MAKES:** 10 servings (3 tablespoons each)

1 cup dark chocolate chips (from 10-oz bag)

1 package (8 oz) cream cheese, softened

2 tablespoons plus 1 teaspoon milk

1/3 cup marshmallow creme (from 7-oz jar)

1/4 cup plus 1½ tablespoons toasted shredded coconut

1 In medium microwavable bowl, microwave chocolate chips, cream cheese and 2 tablespoons milk uncovered on High 40 to 50 seconds, stirring after 20 seconds, until melted.

2 In small bowl, stir marshmallow creme, 1 teaspoon milk and ¼ cup coconut. Spoon ¾ cup of the chocolate mixture into serving bowl; top with marshmallow mixture. Spoon remaining chocolate mixture over marshmallow mixture; with knife, carefully swirl chocolate and marshmallow together. Top with remaining 1½ tablespoons coconut.

1 Serving: Calories 200; Total Fat 14g (Saturated Fat 9g, Trans Fat 0g); Cholesterol 25mg; Sodium 85mg; Total Carbohydrate 16g (Dietary Fiber 1g); Protein 2g **Exchanges:** 1 Other Carbohydrate, 3 Fat **Carbohydrate Choices:** 1

HOW TO STORE: Store covered in the refrigerator up to 5 days. To soften for dipping, uncover and microwave on High 30 to 40 seconds, stirring after 30 seconds, until dipping consistency.

COOKING GLUTEN FREE? Always read labels to make sure *each* recipe ingredient is gluten free. Products and ingredient sources can change.

KITCHEN SECRET: What to serve with this dip? Try it with any of these gluten-free varieties of dippers: graham cracker squares, pretzels, creme wafer squares, mini chocolate creme–filled sandwich cookies, miniature vanilla wafers or bite-size brownies; large vegan marshmallows; toasted almonds, pecans and cashews; or sliced bananas or fresh berries.

KITCHEN SECRET: You can purchase coconut already toasted or toast your own. Spread coconut in an ungreased shallow pan. Bake at 350°F, stirring occasionally, 5 to 7 minutes, or until golden brown.

PEANUT BUTTER–BANANA BITES WITH MINI MARSHMALLOWS

PREP TIME: 5 Minutes ● **START TO FINISH:** 5 Minutes ● **MAKES:** 1 serving

½ medium banana, cut in half lengthwise

1 tablespoon peanut butter

2 tablespoons gluten-free O-shaped toasted honey-nut oat cereal

6 miniature marshmallows, cut in half

Spread each banana slice with peanut butter; top with cereal and marshmallows.

1 Serving: Calories 190; Total Fat 9g (Saturated Fat 2g, Trans Fat 0g); Cholesterol 0mg; Sodium 100mg; Total Carbohydrate 24g (Dietary Fiber 2g); Protein 4g **Exchanges:** ½ Fruit, 1 Other Carbohydrate, ½ High-Fat Meat, 1 Fat **Carbohydrate Choices:** 1½

KITCHEN SECRET: If you use natural peanut butter, remember it can separate or look oily when first opened. Be sure to stir well before using, and store in the refrigerator to prevent separation.

CHANGE IT UP: Almond butter or your favorite nut butter can be substituted for peanut butter for a different flavor.

COOKING GLUTEN FREE? Always read labels to make sure *each* recipe ingredient is gluten free. Products and ingredient sources can change.

HONEY CHAI-SPICED PAN-FRIED BANANAS

PREP TIME: 10 Minutes   •   **START TO FINISH:** 10 Minutes   •   **MAKES:** 2 servings (1 banana each)

2 tablespoons butter
2 tablespoons honey
½ teaspoon ground ginger
¼ teaspoon ground cardamom
¼ teaspoon ground cinnamon
⅛ teaspoon pepper
   Dash ground cloves
2 just-ripe medium bananas,
   cut in half lengthwise

1 In 10-inch nonstick skillet, melt butter over medium heat. Stir in all ingredients except bananas.

2 Place bananas in skillet. Cook 2 to 3 minutes, carefully turning bananas once after about 1 minute with nonstick pancake turner, until bananas are softened and heated through. Remove from heat.

3 Divide bananas and syrup between 2 dessert plates.

1 Serving: Calories 290; Total Fat 12g (Saturated Fat 7g, Trans Fat 0g); Cholesterol 30mg; Sodium 95mg; Total Carbohydrate 45g (Dietary Fiber 3g); Protein 1g **Exchanges:** 1 Fruit, 2 Other Carbohydrate, 2½ Fat **Carbohydrate Choices:** 3

KITCHEN SECRET: Feeling more indulgent? Top the bananas with a dollop of sweetened whipped cream, ice cream or vanilla yogurt and a sprinkle of additional spice.

KITCHEN SECRET: When purchasing bananas, look for bananas that still have a hint of green to them. The firmness of these slightly underripe bananas makes slicing and turning in the pan much easier.

COOKING GLUTEN FREE? Always read labels to make sure *each* recipe ingredient is gluten free. Products and ingredient sources can change.

QUICK PEACH "COBBLER" SNACK

PREP TIME: 5 Minutes   •   **START TO FINISH:** 5 Minutes   •   **MAKES:** 1 serving

- 1 medium peach, cut in half and pitted
- 2 tablespoons light vanilla yogurt
  Dash ground cinnamon
- 2 tablespoons gluten-free O-shaped toasted honey-nut oat cereal

Place peach halves in bowl. Top each peach half with 1 tablespoon yogurt; sprinkle lightly with cinnamon. Top with cereal and serve.

1 Serving: Calories 100; Total Fat 0.5g (Saturated Fat 0g, Trans Fat 0g); Cholesterol 0mg; Sodium 40mg; Total Carbohydrate 21g (Dietary Fiber 2g); Protein 2g **Exchanges:** ½ Starch, 1 Fruit **Carbohydrate Choices:** 1½

CHANGE IT UP: Try peach or another flavor of yogurt for a different taste. Nectarines can also be used in place of the peach.

COOKING GLUTEN FREE? Always read labels to make sure *each* recipe ingredient is gluten free. Products and ingredient sources can change.

SALTED CARAMEL MACCHIATO BROWNIE CUPS

PREP TIME: 10 Minutes • **START TO FINISH:** 1 Hour 40 Minutes • **MAKES:** 12 brownie cups

Foil baking cups
- 1 box (18.4 oz) salted caramel brownie mix
- ⅓ cup vegetable oil
- ¼ cup water
- 1 egg
- 1 tablespoon instant espresso coffee powder
- ½ cup semisweet chocolate chunks (from 11.5-oz bag)
- 1½ cups frozen whipped topping (from 8-oz container), thawed

KITCHEN SECRET: These cups can be enjoyed warm or at room temperature. Sprinkle with unsweetened cocoa powder or top with a few chocolate-covered espresso beans as a garnish.

CHANGE IT UP: Make it a sundae by topping with a scoop of salted caramel, vanilla or coffee ice cream.

1 Heat oven to 350°F. Place foil baking cup in each of 12 regular-size muffin cups; spray bottoms with cooking spray.

2 Make brownie batter as directed on box using oil, water and egg; stir in espresso powder and chocolate chunks until well mixed. Fill each muffin cup with about 2 heaping tablespoons batter.

3 Squeeze salted caramel pouch 10 seconds or until softened. Cut off ¼ inch from corner of pouch. Reserve 1 tablespoon of the caramel topping in a small microwavable bowl; cover and refrigerate until ready to use. Divide remaining caramel equally among muffin cups by squeezing a small amount on top center of brownie batter.

4 Bake 18 to 22 minutes or until edges and tops are set. Cool in pan 5 minutes. Remove from pan; cool completely, at least 1 hour.

5 Just before serving, top each brownie cup with 2 tablespoons whipped topping. Microwave reserved caramel topping uncovered on High 20 to 30 seconds or until drizzling consistency. Place caramel topping in resealable food-storage plastic bag; seal bag. Cut off small corner of bag and drizzle each brownie cup with warm caramel.

1 Brownie Cup: Calories 290; Total Fat 12g (Saturated Fat 5g, Trans Fat 0g); Cholesterol 15mg; Sodium 190mg; Total Carbohydrate 42g (Dietary Fiber 1g); Protein 2g **Exchanges:** ½ Starch, 2½ Other Carbohydrate, 2½ Fat **Carbohydrate Choices:** 3

SPICY CARAMEL CORN SNACK MIX

PREP TIME: 10 Minutes • **START TO FINISH:** 40 Minutes • **MAKES:** 14 servings (½ cup each)

4 cups original flavor horn-shaped corn snacks

1 cup salted roasted whole almonds

⅓ cup caramel topping

1 tablespoon butter, melted

¼ teaspoon ground red pepper (cayenne)

2 cups mini pretzel twists

1 cup unwrapped chocolate-covered chewy caramels (about 28, from 10.6-oz bag)

1 Line 15x10-inch pan with sides with waxed paper; set aside.

2 In large microwavable bowl, place corn snacks and almonds. In small bowl, mix caramel topping, butter and red pepper; pour over corn snack mixture; toss to coat.

3 Microwave uncovered on High 3 to 4 minutes, stirring after every minute, until evenly coated and caramelized. Spread in pan with heat-resistant spatula, separating pieces. Let stand until completely cooled, about 30 minutes.

4 In large serving bowl, toss coated corn snack mixture with pretzels and caramels.

1 Serving: Calories 200; Total Fat 9g (Saturated Fat 3g, Trans Fat 0g); Cholesterol 0mg; Sodium 220mg; Total Carbohydrate 25g (Dietary Fiber 1g); Protein 3g **Exchanges:** 1½ Starch, 1½ Fat **Carbohydrate Choices:** 1½

HOW TO STORE: Store in a covered container at room temperature up to 3 days.

CHANGE IT UP: Notch up the red pepper for more heat. Or add ½ cup sweetened dried cranberries with the pretzels for a delicious twist.

WHITE CHOCOLATE-DRIZZLED CEREAL MIX

PREP TIME: 10 Minutes • **START TO FINISH:** 40 Minutes • **MAKES:** 12 servings (about ½ cup each)

6 cups gluten-free frosted toasted oat cereal with charm-shaped marshmallows

½ cup white vanilla baking chips (from 12-oz bag)

2 tablespoons rainbow-colored nonpareils

1 Line cookie sheet with waxed paper or cooking parchment paper. Spread cereal on cookie sheet.

2 In small microwavable bowl, place vanilla baking chips. Microwave uncovered on High 30 seconds; stir. Continue microwaving in 15-second increments, stirring after every 15 seconds, just until chips start to melt and can be stirred smooth. Transfer to small resealable food-storage plastic bag; seal bag. Cut off small corner of bag and drizzle over cereal. Sprinkle with nonpareils. Let stand until set, about 30 minutes.

1 Serving: Calories 130; Total Fat 3.5g (Saturated Fat 2.5g, Trans Fat 0g); Cholesterol 0mg; Sodium 125mg; Total Carbohydrate 23g (Dietary Fiber 1g); Protein 2g **Exchanges:** 1 Starch, ½ Other Carbohydrate, ½ Fat **Carbohydrate Choices:** 1½

CHANGE IT UP: Extra-hungry? Add some fruit snacks, dried fruit or frosted or plain gluten-free animal crackers.

KITCHEN SECRET: Because of the melt-in-your-mouth marshmallows, this mix is best if eaten the same day it's prepared. If you want a smaller amount, cut the recipe in half.

CHANGE IT UP: Let's celebrate! Serve this in gluten-free ice cream cones to make it special.

COOKING GLUTEN FREE? Always read labels to make sure *each* recipe ingredient is gluten free. Products and ingredient sources can change.

10 Minutes or Less **Sweet**

CELEBRATION SNACK MIX

PREP TIME: 10 Minutes • **START TO FINISH:** 1 Hour 10 Minutes • **MAKES:** 12 servings (about ⅔ cup each)

4 cups bite-size squares oven-toasted rice or corn cereal

4 cups popped popcorn

1 cup creamy white frosting

½ cup white vanilla baking chips (from 12-oz bag)

3 tablespoons assorted candy sprinkles

1 Line cookie sheet with foil or waxed paper.

2 In large bowl, place cereal and popcorn.

3 In medium microwavable bowl, place frosting and baking chips. Microwave uncovered on High about 2 minutes, stirring every 30 seconds, until mixture can be stirred smooth. Pour over cereal mixture; toss to evenly coat.

4 Spread mixture in single layer on cookie sheet. Immediately top with sprinkles. Let stand until set, about 1 hour.

5 Gently break up mixture.

1 Serving: Calories 190; Total Fat 7g (Saturated Fat 3.5g, Trans Fat 0g); Cholesterol 0mg; Sodium 135mg; Total Carbohydrate 30g (Dietary Fiber 0g); Protein 1g **Exchanges:** ½ Starch, 1½ Other Carbohydrate, 1½ Fat **Carbohydrate Choices:** 2

CHANGE IT UP: Use sprinkles that match the color theme of your party. Or for a tailgate party, use sprinkles that are your team's colors!

HOW TO STORE: Store in an airtight container at room temperature up to 2 days.

COOKING GLUTEN FREE? Always read labels to make sure *each* recipe ingredient is gluten free. Products and ingredient sources can change.

20 MINUTES OR LESS

SAVORY

OVEN-BAKED CURRY CHICKEN TAQUITOS

PREP TIME: 15 Minutes • **START TO FINISH:** 30 Minutes • **MAKES:** 4 servings (3 taquitos each)

1¼ cups shredded deli
rotisserie chicken

3 oz cream cheese (from 8-oz
package), softened

3 tablespoons hot mango
chutney (from 9-oz jar),
finely chopped

1½ teaspoons curry powder

⅛ teaspoon salt

12 soft flour tortillas (4½- to 5-inch)

1 tablespoon vegetable oil

1 Heat oven to 400°F. Line 15x10-inch pan with sides with foil.

2 In small bowl, stir together all ingredients except tortillas and oil.

3 Spoon 1 heaping tablespoon of the chicken mixture across center of 1 tortilla. Fold tortilla over filling and tightly roll up. Place seam side down in pan. Repeat with remaining tortillas and chicken mixture, placing them about 1 inch apart in pan. Brush tops and sides generously with oil.

4 Bake 12 to 15 minutes or until golden brown and crispy. Serve immediately.

1 Serving: Calories 350; Total Fat 18g (Saturated Fat 7g, Trans Fat 0g); Cholesterol 60mg; Sodium 720mg; Total Carbohydrate 29g (Dietary Fiber 2g); Protein 17g **Exchanges:** 1½ Starch, ½ Low-Fat Milk, 1 Very Lean Meat, 3 Fat **Carbohydrate Choices:** 2

KITCHEN SECRET: Offer ranch or southwestern dressing as a dip for taquitos. Or place on a serving plate, drizzle with ranch dressing, then sprinkle with chopped fresh cilantro.

KITCHEN SECRET: Look for tortillas that say "soft" on the label. These tortillas will be easier to roll without cracking or splitting. If you can't find them, soften 4 flour tortillas at a time by placing them between damp paper towels on a microwavable plate. Microwave on High 15 to 20 seconds or until warm.

AVOCADO "JALAPEÑO POPPER" BOATS

PREP TIME: 15 Minutes • **START TO FINISH:** 30 Minutes • **MAKES:** 12 boats

1 package (12 count) mini soft flour tortilla taco boats

1 tablespoon butter, melted

1 package (8 oz) cream cheese, softened

2 cans (4.5 oz each) chopped green chiles

1 tablespoon taco seasoning mix (from 1-oz package)

1 ripe avocado, pitted, peeled and diced

1 medium (2- to 3-inch) jalapeño chile, cut in half lengthwise, seeded, very finely chopped

2 teaspoons fresh lime juice

⅛ teaspoon salt

¼ cup crumbled cooked bacon (about 3 slices)

1. Heat oven to 350°F. Line cookie sheet with foil or cooking parchment paper.

2. Brush outsides of boats with melted butter.

3. In medium bowl, mix cream cheese, green chiles and taco seasoning mix with whisk. Divide evenly among boats; spread to smooth top. Place filled boats on cookie sheet. Bake 12 to 14 minutes or until filling is hot and boats are toasted.

4. Meanwhile, in medium bowl, gently mix avocado, jalapeño, lime juice and salt. Spoon avocado mixture into boats. Top with bacon. Serve warm.

1 Boat: Calories 150; Total Fat 11g (Saturated Fat 5g, Trans Fat 0g); Cholesterol 25mg; Sodium 330mg; Total Carbohydrate 10g (Dietary Fiber 1g); Protein 2g **Exchanges:** ½ Starch, 2 Fat **Carbohydrate Choices:** ½

KITCHEN SECRET: To dice avocado, cut avocado lengthwise through skin and flesh around pit. Slowly twist both sides of avocado to separate. Gently slide spoon under pit to remove. With a knife, make crisscross cuts through flesh; remove with spoon into bowl.

BACON JALAPEÑO TURKEY ROLL-UPS

PREP TIME: 20 Minutes • **START TO FINISH:** 2 Hours 20 Minutes • **MAKES:** 12 slices

- 4 oz (half of 8-oz package) cream cheese, softened
- ½ teaspoon ground cumin
- ½ teaspoon ground coriander
- ⅛ teaspoon ground red pepper (cayenne)
- 2 large (10-inch) spinach tortillas
- ¼ cup crumbled cooked bacon (about 3 slices)
- 1 tablespoon chopped drained pickled jalapeño chile slices
- 5 oz thinly sliced deli turkey
- 4 mozzarella cheese sticks

1 In medium bowl, mix cream cheese, cumin, coriander and red pepper. Divide mixture between tortillas, spreading to edges of tortillas. Top evenly with bacon and jalapeños. Top with deli turkey. Place 2 cheese sticks at one edge of each tortilla, end to end. Roll up very tightly. Cover with plastic wrap. Refrigerate at least 2 hours but no longer than 24 hours.

2 To serve, cut each roll into 6 (½-inch) slices.

1 Slice: Calories 110; Total Fat 6g (Saturated Fat 3g, Trans Fat 0g); Cholesterol 25mg; Sodium 290mg; Total Carbohydrate 6g (Dietary Fiber 0g); Protein 6g **Exchanges:** ½ Starch, ½ Medium-Fat Meat, ½ Fat **Carbohydrate Choices:** ½

KITCHEN SECRET: The jalapeño slices and red pepper give these roll-ups a nice kick, but if you like it hotter, increase the red pepper to ¼ teaspoon.

CHANGE IT UP: For a fun twist, use smoked mozzarella cheese sticks.

KIMCHI-CHICKEN QUESADILLAS

PREP TIME: 20 Minutes • **START TO FINISH:** 30 Minutes • **MAKES:** 4 servings (3 wedges each)

GOCHUJANG MAYONNAISE

- ⅓ cup mayonnaise
- 2 teaspoons gochujang (Korean chili paste)
- 1 teaspoon toasted sesame seed

QUESADILLAS

- 1½ cups shredded deli rotisserie chicken
- 1 cup kimchi (from 16-oz jar), well drained, chopped
- ¼ cup thinly sliced green onions (4 medium)
- 1 tablespoon vegetable oil
- 4 burrito-size flour tortillas (8-inch)
- 1½ cups finely shredded Cheddar-Jack cheese (6 oz)

1. In small bowl, stir together Gochujang Mayonnaise ingredients; cover and refrigerate until ready to serve.

2. In medium microwavable bowl, mix chicken and kimchi. Microwave covered on High 1 minute to 1 minute 30 seconds or until heated through. Stir in onions.

3. Heat nonstick griddle over medium-low heat. Brush one side of 2 of the tortillas with some of the oil; place tortillas oil side down on griddle, 2 inches apart. Top each tortilla with ⅓ cup of the cheese. Top with chicken mixture, spreading it evenly over cheese. Sprinkle each with remaining cheese, divided equally; top with another tortilla. Brush tops of tortillas with remaining oil.

4. Cook for 4 to 6 minutes, turning once, until tortillas are golden brown and crisp and cheese is melted. Cut each quesadilla into 6 wedges. Serve with Gochujang Mayonnaise.

1 Serving: Calories 580; Total Fat 39g (Saturated Fat 13g, Trans Fat 0.5g); Cholesterol 95mg; Sodium 1020mg; Total Carbohydrate 28g (Dietary Fiber 2g); Protein 30g **Exchanges:** 1½ Starch, ½ Vegetable, 2 Lean Meat, 1½ High-Fat Meat, 4 Fat **Carbohydrate Choices:** 2

CHANGE IT UP: Kimchi, a spicy pickled cabbage mixture, comes in mild and hot varieties. It's also a great addition to your favorite stir-fry or grain bowl.

KITCHEN SECRET: Gochujang is Korean chili paste, a spicy fermented condiment commonly found in the Asian aisle of the grocery store; it is sold as a paste or a sauce. It can vary in flavor and heat level. You can substitute 2 teaspoons sriracha for the gochujang. It will give the spiciness but not the depth of flavor that gochujang offers.

KITCHEN SECRET: If you like, arrange quesadilla wedges on a platter with the Gochujang Mayonnaise in a bowl in the center. Garnish with additional sliced green onions or chopped fresh Italian flat-leaf parsley.

CHEESY BEEF AND GREEN CHILE SPICY TACOS

PREP TIME: 15 Minutes • **START TO FINISH:** 25 Minutes • **MAKES:** 5 tacos

½ lb ground beef (at least 80% lean)

2 tablespoons original taco seasoning mix (from 1-oz package)

2 tablespoons water

¼ cup drained chopped green chiles (from 4.5-oz can)

5 spicy taco shells

½ cup shredded sharp cheddar cheese (2 oz)

2 tablespoons sour cream

2 tablespoons thinly sliced green onions (2 medium)

1. In 10-inch nonstick skillet, cook beef over medium heat 4 to 5 minutes, stirring occasionally, until thoroughly cooked; drain. Stir in taco seasoning mix, water and green chiles. Cook 30 to 60 seconds longer or until liquid is absorbed.

2. Heat shells as directed on package. Serve with beef mixture, cheese, sour cream and green onions.

1 Taco: Calories 220; Total Fat 14g (Saturated Fat 7g, Trans Fat 0g); Cholesterol 40mg; Sodium 400mg; Total Carbohydrate 12g (Dietary Fiber 0g); Protein 11g **Exchanges:** 1 Other Carbohydrate, 1 Lean Meat, ½ High-Fat Meat, 1½ Fat **Carbohydrate Choices:** 1

KITCHEN SECRET: Your choice of toppings is limitless! Try sliced fresh jalapeño chiles, diced tomato, guacamole, shredded lettuce, fresh cilantro leaves and/or lime wedges.

KITCHEN SECRET: For a pretty sour cream topping, spoon some into a small resealable food-storage plastic bag; seal bag. Cut off a tiny corner and squeeze a zigzag of sour cream on top of each taco.

CHICK PEA AND VEGGIE BURGERS

PREP TIME: 20 Minutes • **START TO FINISH:** 20 Minutes • **MAKES:** 4 sandwiches

½ cup fresh broccoli florets

2 oz fresh whole mushrooms (about 4 medium)

½ small red bell pepper, cut into large pieces

½ cup cooked white or brown rice

1 can (15 to 16 oz) chick peas or garbanzo beans, drained, rinsed

1 egg

1 clove garlic, peeled

½ teaspoon seasoned salt

1 teaspoon dried chopped onion

⅓ cup seasoned dry bread crumbs

3 tablespoons vegetable oil

4 hamburger or other buns, split

1 In food processor, place broccoli, mushrooms and bell pepper. Cover; process, using quick on-and-off motions, to finely chop vegetables (do not puree). Transfer vegetables from processor to medium bowl; stir in rice.

2 Place beans, egg, garlic and seasoned salt in food processor. Cover; process until smooth. Stir bean mixture, dried chopped onion and bread crumbs into vegetable mixture. Shape mixture into 4 patties, about ½ inch thick.

3 In 10-inch nonstick skillet, heat oil over medium-high heat. Cook patties in oil 8 to 10 minutes, turning once, until brown and crisp. Serve in buns.

1 Sandwich: Calories 400; Total Fat 16g (Saturated Fat 2.5g, Trans Fat 0g); Cholesterol 45mg; Sodium 690mg; Total Carbohydrate 51g (Dietary Fiber 6g); Protein 13g **Exchanges:** 3 Other Carbohydrate, 1 Vegetable, 1½ Very Lean Meat, 3 Fat **Carbohydrate Choices:** 3½

CHANGE IT UP: Top these burgers with the regular burger toppings, such as slices of red onion and tomato with lettuce, or try something different like tzatziki sauce, smashed avocado, kimchi and a fried egg, or potato chips!

CRAB CAKE BITES

PREP TIME: 20 Minutes • **START TO FINISH:** 45 Minutes • **MAKES:** 36 servings (1 bite and about 1 teaspoon sauce each)

CRAB CAKES

- ½ cup mayonnaise
- 1 egg
- 2 tablespoons chopped fresh chives
- 1 teaspoon Worcestershire sauce
- 1 teaspoon Dijon mustard
- 1½ teaspoons seafood seasoning (from 6-oz container)
- 1 teaspoon fresh lemon juice
- 2 containers (8 oz each) refrigerated pasteurized lump crabmeat, cleaned
- ⅔ cup plain panko crispy bread crumbs

LEMON-GARLIC SAUCE

- 1 cup mayonnaise
- 2 teaspoons Dijon mustard
- 2 teaspoons fresh lemon juice
- 1 teaspoon finely chopped garlic
- ¼ teaspoon salt

1 Heat oven to 400°F. Line large cookie sheet with cooking parchment paper.

2 To make Crab Cakes, in medium bowl, stir together all ingredients except crabmeat and bread crumbs. Gently toss in crabmeat and bread crumbs until well blended (mixture will be moist). Using measuring tablespoon, shape mixture into 36 (1½-inch) balls. Place on cookie sheet.

3 Bake 16 to 20 minutes or until lightly browned and hot in center. Cool 5 minutes.

4 Meanwhile, in small bowl, stir together Lemon-Garlic Sauce ingredients until blended. Serve bites with sauce.

1 Serving: Calories 80; Total Fat 7g (Saturated Fat 1g, Trans Fat 0g); Cholesterol 20mg; Sodium 190mg; Total Carbohydrate 2g (Dietary Fiber 0g); Protein 2g **Exchanges:** ½ Lean Meat, 1 Fat **Carbohydrate Choices:** 0

KITCHEN SECRET: These bites are ready to party, served up with the sauce and topped with sliced green onion and lemon slices on the side!

KITCHEN SECRET: For even baking, make sure the crab mixture balls are the same shape and size.

HERBED GOAT CHEESE PIZZA POPPERS

PREP TIME: 15 Minutes • **START TO FINISH:** 15 Minutes • **MAKES:** 8 servings (2 bell pepper halves each)

1 package (4 oz) plain chèvre (goat) cheese, softened

¾ cup shredded mozzarella cheese (3 oz)

1½ teaspoons chopped fresh thyme leaves

8 mini bell peppers, cut in half lengthwise, seeded, stems intact

¼ cup gluten-free pizza sauce (from 14-oz jar)

1) Set oven control to broil; position oven rack 6 inches from broiler. Line 15×10×1-inch pan with foil.

2) In medium bowl, place goat cheese, ¼ cup of the mozzarella cheese and the thyme; mix well. Spoon mixture into pepper halves, dividing equally. Top peppers with remaining ½ cup mozzarella cheese, divided evenly. Place peppers in pan.

3) Broil 1 to 1½ minutes or until cheese is melted and starting to brown.

4) Drizzle with pizza sauce; serve immediately.

1 Serving: Calories 100; Total Fat 7g (Saturated Fat 4g, Trans Fat 0g); Cholesterol 20mg; Sodium 160mg; Total Carbohydrate 4g (Dietary Fiber 1g); Protein 6g **Exchanges:** ½ Vegetable, ½ Medium-Fat Meat, 1 Fat **Carbohydrate Choices:** 0

KITCHEN SECRET: Mini bell peppers come in different shapes and sizes. We selected peppers that were about 3 inches long and wide enough to be easily filled with the cheese mixture.

KITCHEN SECRET: Assemble the peppers ahead of time and refrigerate until ready to broil, then serve for a quick party appetizer!

COOKING GLUTEN FREE? Always read labels to make sure *each* recipe ingredient is gluten free. Products and ingredient sources can change.

CHANGE IT UP: Fresh basil is a colorful topper for these delicious peppers. Other fresh herbs can be substituted for the thyme; simply use what you have on hand. If you don't have fresh herbs, substitute ½ teaspoon of the dried herb instead. You can also substitute herbed goat cheese or soft garlic-and-herbs cheese for the goat cheese and thyme for an equally delicious—and easy—alternative!

OVEN-TOASTED RAVIOLI

PREP TIME: 20 Minutes • **START TO FINISH:** 40 Minutes • **MAKES:** 6 servings

1 egg

1 tablespoon water

1 cup Italian-style panko crispy bread crumbs

⅓ cup grated Parmesan cheese

1 package (9 oz) refrigerated cheese-filled ravioli

1 cup jarred Alfredo pasta sauce

1 Heat oven to 400°F. Line 15x10x1-inch pan with foil. Place 15×10-inch wire cooling rack on top of foil; spray with cooking spray.

2 In small bowl, beat egg and water with whisk. In shallow dish or pie plate, mix bread crumbs and cheese.

3 Dip each ravioli into egg mixture, then into bread crumb mixture, pressing crumbs lightly to adhere to ravioli; place on rack in single layer, not touching.

4 Bake 15 to 20 minutes or until ravioli are crispy and edges are slightly browned.

5 Meanwhile, pour Alfredo sauce into microwavable dish; loosely cover. Microwave on High 30 seconds. Stir, then microwave about 15 seconds longer or until warm. Serve with ravioli.

1 Serving: Calories 370; Total Fat 20g (Saturated Fat 12g, Trans Fat 0.5g); Cholesterol 100mg; Sodium 720mg; Total Carbohydrate 35g (Dietary Fiber 0g); Protein 12g **Exchanges:** 2½ Starch, ½ Lean Meat, 3½ Fat **Carbohydrate Choices:** 2

CHANGE IT UP: If you don't have Alfredo sauce on hand, try using your favorite marinara sauce or pesto for dipping—or pick two sauces and dip the ravioli in both!

KITCHEN SECRET: Using a wire rack in this recipe helps toast the ravioli on both sides without turning.

KITCHEN SECRET: Hands can get so messy when breading! Try this easy way to bread ravioli or other foods: Use one hand (wet hand) to dip ravioli into the egg mixture; shake off excess egg, then place in the bread crumbs. Use your other hand (dry hand) to coat the ravioli in crumbs and place on the rack.

BASIL-CHEESE TRIANGLES

PREP TIME: 15 Minutes • **START TO FINISH:** 30 Minutes • **MAKES:** 18 triangles

1 cup crumbled feta cheese (4 oz)

1 egg, slightly beaten

1 tablespoon finely chopped fresh or 1 teaspoon dried basil leaves

5 (18×14-inch) sheets (¼ of 16-oz package) frozen phyllo (filo), thawed

3 tablespoons butter, melted

1 Heat oven to 400°F. Spray cookie sheet with cooking spray.

2 In small bowl, mash cheese with fork to break up large crumbles. Stir in egg and basil until well mixed.

3 Cut phyllo sheets lengthwise into 2-inch-wide strips. (Cover with plastic wrap, then with damp towel, to keep them from drying out.) Place 1 level teaspoon of the cheese mixture on end of 1 strip. Fold strip over cheese mixture, end over end in triangular shape, to opposite end. Place on cookie sheet seam side down. Repeat with remaining phyllo strips and cheese mixture. Brush triangles lightly with butter.

4 Bake 12 to 15 minutes or until puffed and golden brown. Serve warm.

1 Triangle: Calories 50; Total Fat 3g (Saturated Fat 1.5g, Trans Fat 0g); Cholesterol 20mg; Sodium 105mg; Total Carbohydrate 4g (Dietary Fiber 0g); Protein 1g **Exchanges:** ½ Starch, ½ Fat **Carbohydrate Choices:** 0

CHANGE IT UP: Here are a couple customized options for these triangles: Substitute finely shredded Monterey Jack cheese for the feta cheese and/or chopped fresh or freeze-dried chives for the basil.

KITCHEN SECRET: Cover and refrigerate unbaked triangles up to 24 hours before baking; bake as directed. Or freeze, tightly covered, up to 2 months; increase bake time by 5 minutes.

LOADED PIZZA SCRAMBLED EGGS

PREP TIME: 15 Minutes • **START TO FINISH:** 25 Minutes • **MAKES:** 3 servings (½ slice bread and ½ cup eggs each)

1 tablespoon butter

½ cup chopped red bell pepper

⅓ cup sliced pepperoni minis (from 5-oz pouch)

⅓ cup frozen pork sausage crumbles (from 9.6-oz bag)

¼ cup sliced green onions (4 medium)

6 eggs

2 tablespoons water

⅛ teaspoon salt

⅛ teaspoon pepper

¾ cup shredded Parmesan cheese (3 oz)

½ cup shredded Italian cheese blend (2 oz)

6 tablespoons pizza or marinara sauce, heated

3 large slices bread, such as Italian or sourdough, toasted

① In 10-inch nonstick skillet, melt butter over medium-high heat. Add bell pepper, pepperoni, sausage and green onions; cook 1 to 2 minutes or until pepper is crisp-tender and sausage is thoroughly heated.

② In medium bowl, beat eggs, water, salt and pepper with fork or whisk until well mixed. Pour eggs over sausage mixture. Cook uncovered 3 to 4 minutes, stirring occasionally, until thoroughly cooked and eggs are set but moist. Stir in cheeses; cook 1 to 2 minutes longer or until cheeses are melted.

③ Spread 2 tablespoons of the pizza sauce on each toasted bread slice. Top each bread slice with about 1 cup of the egg mixture; cut in half. Serve immediately.

1 Serving: Calories 290; Total Fat 19g (Saturated Fat 9g, Trans Fat 0g); Cholesterol 220mg; Sodium 700mg; Total Carbohydrate 11g (Dietary Fiber 1g); Protein 17g **Exchanges:** 2 Medium-Fat Meat **Carbohydrate Choices:** 1

CHANGE IT UP: Sprinkle each serving with sliced fresh basil leaves or sliced green onions.

KITCHEN SECRET: If you love sauce, top your eggs with additional pizza sauce. Yum!

LOADED BAKED POTATO NACHOS

PREP TIME: 15 Minutes • **START TO FINISH:** 15 Minutes • **MAKES:** 3 servings

1½ tablespoons butter, melted

1½ teaspoons gluten-free dry ranch dressing mix (from 1-oz package)

2 cups gluten-free bite-size squares oven-toasted corn cereal

2 cups potato chips (1.4 oz)

1 cup shredded cheddar cheese (4 oz)

4 slices gluten-free bacon, crisply cooked, crumbled (about ⅓ cup)

2 tablespoons gluten-free ranch dressing

1½ teaspoons chopped fresh chives

1 Heat oven to 400°F. Line 13×9-inch pan with cooking parchment paper.

2 In large bowl, mix melted butter and ranch dressing mix. Add cereal; toss to coat. Spread mixture in single layer in pan.

3 Bake 3 minutes. Stir in potato chips. Sprinkle evenly with cheese and bacon. Bake 3 to 4 minutes or until cheese is melted.

4 Drizzle with the ranch dressing; sprinkle with chives. Serve immediately.

1 Serving: Calories 460; Total Fat 32g (Saturated Fat 13g, Trans Fat 0.5g); Cholesterol 65mg; Sodium 990mg; Total Carbohydrate 28g (Dietary Fiber 1g); Protein 15g **Exchanges:** 1½ Starch, ½ Other Carbohydrate, 1½ High-Fat Meat, 4 Fat **Carbohydrate Choices:** 2

CHANGE IT UP: With so many different flavors of potato chips, customize these nachos to your liking or use what you have on hand. Try sour cream and chive, barbecue, cheddar or dill pickle–flavored chips, or a combination of several flavors.

COOKING GLUTEN FREE? Always read labels to make sure *each* recipe ingredient is gluten free. Products and ingredient sources can change.

GRILLED BEAN CHIP NACHOS

PREP TIME: 15 Minutes • **START TO FINISH:** 15 Minutes • **MAKES:** 8 servings (2 tablespoons each)

2½ cups black bean multigrain chips (from 5.5-oz bag)

1 cup shredded Monterey Jack cheese (4 oz)

¼ cup chopped green chiles (from 4.5-oz can)

1 avocado, pitted, peeled and diced

1 plum (Roma) tomato, chopped

1 Heat gas or charcoal grill. Spray 13×9-inch foil pan with cooking spray. Spread chips in single layer in pan; sprinkle with cheese and green chiles. Cover pan with foil.

2 Place pan on grill over medium heat. Cover grill; cook 8 to 10 minutes or until cheese is melted. Carefully remove foil. Top nachos with avocado and tomato. Serve warm.

1 Serving: Calories 130; Total Fat 9g (Saturated Fat 3g, Trans Fat 0g); Cholesterol 15mg; Sodium 135mg; Total Carbohydrate 8g (Dietary Fiber 2g); Protein 5g **Exchanges:** ½ Starch, ½ High-Fat Meat, 1 Fat **Carbohydrate Choices:** ½

KITCHEN SECRET: Serve these nachos with sour cream and a drizzle of your favorite hot sauce.

BEER QUESO NACHOS

PREP TIME: 20 Minutes • **START TO FINISH:** 20 Minutes • **MAKES:** 12 servings

8 cups tortilla chips

½ cup lager (light) beer

2 cups shredded American cheese (8 oz)

1 cup shredded mild cheddar cheese (4 oz)

1 can (4.5 oz) chopped green chiles, drained

1 can (15 oz) black beans, drained, rinsed

½ cup chunky salsa

1 medium avocado, pitted, peeled and chopped

1 medium tomato, seeded, chopped

2 tablespoons chopped fresh cilantro

1 Heat oven to 350°F. Line large cookie sheet with cooking parchment paper.

2 Arrange tortilla chips in single layer on cookie sheet. Bake 5 minutes or until warm.

3 Meanwhile, in 2-quart saucepan, heat beer over medium heat just until starting to simmer. Slowly add cheeses in small amounts, stirring constantly with whisk, until melted. Stir in chiles.

4 In medium microwavable bowl, mix beans and salsa. Microwave uncovered on High 2 to 3 minutes or until hot, stirring occasionally.

5 To serve, transfer warm chips to large serving platter. Top evenly with half of the cheese sauce, then half of the bean mixture. Repeat with remaining cheese sauce and bean mixture. Sprinkle with avocado, tomato and cilantro.

1 Serving: Calories 280; Total Fat 16g (Saturated Fat 7g, Trans Fat 0g); Cholesterol 30mg; Sodium 580mg; Total Carbohydrate 23g (Dietary Fiber 4g); Protein 10g **Exchanges:** 1 Starch, ½ Other Carbohydrate, 1 High-Fat Meat, 1½ Fat **Carbohydrate Choices:** 1½

KITCHEN SECRET: Boost your veggies by piling on vegetables such as shredded lettuce, chopped onion and chopped bell pepper.

LOADED CHICKEN TOTCHOS

PREP TIME: 15 Minutes   •   **START TO FINISH:** 50 Minutes   •   **MAKES:** 8 servings

1 bag (32 oz) frozen potato nuggets

1 can (4.5 oz) chopped green chiles, drained

2 tablespoons vegetable oil

2 tablespoons water

1 package (0.85 oz) chicken taco seasoning mix

2 cups shredded deli rotisserie chicken

2 cups shredded Mexican cheese blend (8 oz)

¼ cup sour cream

2 medium plum (Roma) tomatoes, diced

2 tablespoons chopped fresh cilantro leaves

1 Heat oven to 425°F. Line 15x10-inch pan with sides with cooking parchment paper.

2 Spread potato nuggets in pan. Bake as directed on bag, stirring halfway through.

3 Meanwhile, in medium bowl, mix chiles, oil, water and taco seasoning mix. Stir in chicken.

4 Sprinkle potatoes evenly with 1 cup of the cheese. Top with chicken mixture; top with remaining 1 cup cheese. Bake 7 to 9 minutes longer or until cheese is melted and chicken mixture is hot.

5 Top with sour cream, tomatoes and cilantro.

1 Serving: Calories 460; Total Fat 29g (Saturated Fat 10g, Trans Fat 0g); Cholesterol 60mg; Sodium 1120mg; Total Carbohydrate 32g (Dietary Fiber 3g); Protein 19g **Exchanges:** 1½ Starch, ½ Other Carbohydrate, 1 Lean Meat, 1 High-Fat Meat, 3½ Fat **Carbohydrate Choices:** 2

KITCHEN SECRET: If you like your nuggets really crispy, add 5 minutes to the initial bake time.

KITCHEN SECRET: For an easy way to drizzle sour cream, spoon into a small resealable plastic food-storage bag; seal bag. Cut off ¼ inch from a corner and squeeze sour cream over the totchos.

FETA AND SPINACH-STUFFED BREAD

PREP TIME: 15 Minutes • **START TO FINISH:** 40 Minutes • **MAKES:** 6 slices

1½ oz thinly sliced prosciutto (from 3-oz package), cut crosswise into ¼-inch strips

½ loaf French bread (8 oz)

1 cup shredded mozzarella cheese (4 oz)

⅓ cup chopped red bell pepper

½ cup chopped fresh baby spinach leaves

½ teaspoon garlic powder

1 package (4 oz) crumbled feta cheese

2 oz cream cheese (from 8-oz package), softened

⅓ cup shredded Parmesan cheese (a little under 3 oz)

1 Heat oven to 350°F. Line large cookie sheet with cooking parchment paper.

2 In 10-inch nonstick skillet, cook prosciutto over medium-high heat, stirring occasionally, 4 to 5 minutes or until crisp.

3 Place bread on cookie sheet. Using a serrated knife, carefully hollow out bread by cutting a 3-inch-wide V shape lengthwise down center of loaf to within ½ inch of bottom.

4 In medium bowl, stir together prosciutto and remaining ingredients except Parmesan cheese until well mixed. Spoon cheese mixture into hollowed-out loaf; sprinkle with Parmesan cheese.

5 Bake 20 to 22 minutes or until filling is hot and cheeses are melted. Cool 5 minutes.

6 Cut into slices and serve warm.

1 Slice: Calories 280; Total Fat 14g (Saturated Fat 8g, Trans Fat 0g); Cholesterol 45mg; Sodium 770mg; Total Carbohydrate 23g (Dietary Fiber 1g); Protein 15g **Exchanges:** 1½ Starch, 1½ Medium-Fat Meat, 1 Fat **Carbohydrate Choices:** 1½

CHANGE IT UP: Don't have prosciutto on hand? You can substitute 6 slices crumbled crisply cooked bacon or 3 tablespoons cooked real bacon bits for the prosciutto.

KITCHEN SECRET: Serve this cheesy bread as a game day appetizer, or serve with your favorite chili, soup or pasta.

FRENCH BREAD TACO PIZZA

PREP TIME: 20 Minutes • **START TO FINISH:** 30 Minutes • **MAKES:** 4 servings

1 loaf French bread (1 lb)

½ lb ground beef (at least 80% lean)

2 tablespoons original taco seasoning mix (from 1-oz package)

⅓ cup water

1 can (16 oz) refried beans

1 yellow bell pepper, cut into ¾-inch pieces

½ cup thinly sliced red onion

1½ cups shredded Mexican cheese blend (6 oz)

1 cup shredded lettuce

1 tomato, chopped

1. Heat oven to 425°F. Line large cookie sheet with foil.

2. Cut bread in half lengthwise, then in half crosswise. Place on cookie sheet cut sides up. Bake about 5 minutes or until lightly toasted.

3. In 8-inch skillet, cook beef over medium-high heat, stirring frequently, until thoroughly cooked; drain. Add taco seasoning mix and water; cook until thickened.

4. Spread refried beans over toasted bread. Top with beef mixture, bell pepper, onion and cheese. Bake 10 to 12 minutes or until cheese is melted. Top with lettuce and tomato.

1 Serving: Calories 710; Total Fat 24g (Saturated Fat 12g, Trans Fat 1g); Cholesterol 75mg; Sodium 1540mg; Total Carbohydrate 86g (Dietary Fiber 8g); Protein 38g **Exchanges:** 2 Starch, 3½ Other Carbohydrate, ½ Vegetable, 1 Very Lean Meat, 2 Medium-Fat Meat, 1½ High-Fat Meat **Carbohydrate Choices:** 6

KITCHEN SECRET: Use any of your favorite taco ingredients and layer them on top of the bread. Spoon on salsa or guacamole, drizzle with sour cream and sprinkle with ripe olives or slivers of red onion.

KITCHEN SECRET: For a quick and easy dinner, cook the ground beef mixture ahead and refrigerate. At dinner time, just top the bread and bake.

MINI HOT DOG-PIMIENTO CHEESE BITES

PREP TIME: 20 Minutes • **START TO FINISH:** 30 Minutes • **MAKES:** 12 servings (1 bite and 1 tablespoon dip each)

PIMIENTO CHEESE

- 1 cup shredded cheddar cheese (4 oz)
- ¼ cup mayonnaise
- 2 tablespoons drained chopped pimientos (from 2-oz jar)
- 2 oz cream cheese (from 8-oz package), softened
- 5 drops red pepper sauce
- 1 tablespoon milk

BITES

- 4 slices soft sandwich bread
- 12 cocktail-size smoked link sausages (from 14-oz package)
- 1 tablespoon butter, melted
- ¼ teaspoon dried dill weed

1 Heat oven to 400°F. Line cookie sheet with cooking parchment paper.

2 In small microwavable bowl, mix all Pimiento Cheese ingredients except milk.

3 Cut crusts from bread; flatten bread slices with rolling pin. Spread each slice with 1½ tablespoons of the Pimiento Cheese; reserve remaining Pimiento Cheese for dip.

4 Cut each slice into 3 rectangles with sharp knife. Place a sausage on one end of each rectangle; roll up. Place rolls seam side down on cookie sheet. In small bowl, mix butter and dill weed; brush over each roll-up.

5 Bake for 7 to 8 minutes or until edges are golden brown.

6 Meanwhile, stir milk into remaining Pimiento Cheese.

7 Just before serving, microwave cheese mixture uncovered on High 30 seconds or until warm. Serve dip with bites.

1 Serving: Calories 90; Total Fat 8g (Saturated Fat 3.5g, Trans Fat 0g); Cholesterol 15mg; Sodium 130mg; Total Carbohydrate 0g (Dietary Fiber 0g); Protein 2g **Exchanges:** ½ Medium-Fat Meat, 1 Fat **Carbohydrate Choices:** 0

KITCHEN SECRET: Offset metal spatulas are great for fast and easy spreading. An offset spatula has an angled blade that helps you spread without getting your fingers into whatever you're spreading.

KITCHEN SECRET: You can use any soft bread to make these bites. Sandwich bread is rectangular in shape, making less waste when the crusts are trimmed. Use the crusts to make dry or toasted bread crumbs to top egg and vegetable dishes or even salads.

SLOW-COOKER BOURBON-HONEY BBQ WINGS

PREP TIME: 15 Minutes • **START TO FINISH:** 2 Hours 25 Minutes • **MAKES:** 12 servings (2 wing pieces each)

1 bottle (12 oz) gluten-free sweet and spicy barbecue sauce

¼ cup honey

6 teaspoons bourbon

2 lb chicken wings and drummettes

1 In small bowl, stir together barbecue sauce, honey and 5 teaspoons of the bourbon. In 6-quart slow cooker, place wings in single layer. Pour barbecue sauce mixture over wings. Cover; cook on High heat setting 2 to 2½ hours or until juice of chicken is clear when thickest part is cut to bone (at least 175°F).

2 Set oven control to broil. Line 15x10x1-inch pan with foil. Place 15x10-inch wire cooling rack on top of foil.

3 Transfer wings to rack. Broil wings 5 to 6 minutes or until coating is bubbly and slightly darkened.

4 Meanwhile, spoon fat off barbecue sauce mixture; transfer to 2-quart saucepan. Heat to simmering over medium-high heat. Cook 5 to 6 minutes or until slightly thickened. Remove from heat; stir in remaining 1 teaspoon bourbon.

5 Transfer wings to serving platter. Drizzle wings with some of the barbecue sauce; serve remaining sauce on the side.

1 Serving: Calories 150; Total Fat 4.5g (Saturated Fat 1.5g, Trans Fat 0g); Cholesterol 45mg; Sodium 260mg; Total Carbohydrate 18g (Dietary Fiber 0g); Protein 8g **Exchanges:** 1 Other Carbohydrate, 1 Lean Meat, ½ Fat **Carbohydrate Choices:** 1

KITCHEN SECRET: Using a 6-quart slow cooker provides enough surface area for the wings to be arranged in a single layer. This allows them to cook without falling apart in the sauce. Cooking wings to 175°F ensures the meat will easily come off the bone.

COOKING GLUTEN FREE? Always read labels to make sure *each* recipe ingredient is gluten free. Products and ingredient sources can change.

FLAKY DELI SLICES

PREP TIME: 15 Minutes • **START TO FINISH:** 35 Minutes • **MAKES:** 16 slices

1 refrigerated pie crust (from 14.1-oz box), softened as directed on box

2 tablespoons grated Parmesan cheese

6 oz very thinly sliced cooked ham

½ cup thinly sliced pepperoni

½ cup shredded cheddar cheese (2 oz)

1 Heat oven to 450°F.

2 Unroll crust. Sprinkle evenly with Parmesan cheese; top with ham, pepperoni and cheddar cheese to within 1 inch of edge. Loosely roll up crust. Place roll, seam side down, on ungreased cookie sheet. Fold ends under.

3 Bake 12 to 17 minutes or until golden brown. Cool 5 minutes.

4 Cut into 16 slices. Serve warm.

1 Slice: Calories 110; Total Fat 7g (Saturated Fat 3g, Trans Fat 0g); Cholesterol 15mg; Sodium 330mg; Total Carbohydrate 6g (Dietary Fiber 0g); Protein 5g **Exchanges:** ½ Starch, ½ High-Fat Meat, ½ Fat **Carbohydrate Choices:** ½

CHANGE IT UP: You can substitute your favorite sliced deli meat for the pepperoni. Make it all ham, ham and turkey, salami and ham or other variations. The cheese can also be changed based on what you have on hand.

ROASTED BEANS 3 WAYS

You'll hug yourself when you reach for a handful of these snacks instead of chips. Not only are they a plant-based snack, but they are a good source of protein as well.

Crunchy roasted beans are a great snack any time of day! Go beyond chick peas—did you know you can roast other beans as well?

ROASTING TIPS

- **PICK** a bean type and seasoning blend.

- **RINSE,** drain and dry beans well to get the crunchiest snack.

- **COVER YOURSELF** Hot beans can jump as they crisp! Use an oven mitt to cover your hand when stirring and removing pan from oven.

- **ROAST** beans for the minimum time; add additional time if needed.

- **ARE THEY DONE?** Test for desired crunch and texture by removing a few beans from various locations on pan; let cool before tasting. Beans crisp up more as they cool, and bigger beans take longer to crisp.

- **STORE** roasted beans in a bowl loosely covered with waxed paper at room temperature up to 5 days.

- **ENJOY** Eat the beans out of your hand or use them as a fun topper for hummus or other savory dips or toss in your favorite salad.

Roasted Beans
3 Ways recipe on
the next page

147

ROASTED BEANS 3 WAYS

PREP TIME: 10 Minutes   •   **START TO FINISH:** 1 Hour 30 Minutes   •   **MAKES:** About 5 servings (⅓ cup each)

BEANS

- 2 cans (15 oz each) chick peas or garbanzo beans, butter beans or cannellini beans, rinsed and drained
- 2 tablespoons vegetable oil

SMOKY MEXICAN SEASONING BLEND

- 1 teaspoon ground chipotle chile pepper
- 1 teaspoon grated lime zest
- ½ teaspoon salt
- ½ teaspoon ground cumin

EASY INDIAN SEASONING BLEND

- 2 teaspoons garam masala
- ½ teaspoon salt

ITALIAN HERB SEASONING BLEND

- 2 teaspoons gluten-free Italian seasoning
- ½ teaspoon garlic salt

1. Heat oven to 400°F. Place beans on several thicknesses of paper towels and blot dry.

2. In medium bowl, stir together vegetable oil and ingredients for one of the Seasoning Blends. Stir in beans until evenly coated. Place beans in single layer on 15x10-inch pan with sides.

3. Bake 45 to 60 minutes, stirring every 15 minutes, until beans are deep golden brown, dry and crunchy. Let cool in pan at least 15 minutes.

1 Serving (Smoky Mexican Chick Peas) Calories 210; Total Fat 9g (Saturated Fat 1g, Trans Fat 0g); Cholesterol 0mg; Sodium 500mg; Total Carbohydrate 25g (Dietary Fiber 7g); Protein 7g **Exchanges:** 1 Starch, ½ Other Carbohydrate, ½ Very Lean Meat, 1½ Fat **Carbohydrate Choices:** 1½

HOW TO STORE: Store in a bowl, loosely covered with waxed paper, at room temperature up to 5 days.

KITCHEN SECRET: Be sure to bake the beans for the minimum time; add more time if necessary. To check for doneness, remove a few beans from various locations in the pan; cool. Taste for desired crunch and texture. You can always pop them back in the oven until you get the crunch you like. Keep in mind that larger beans will take longer to crisp.

KITCHEN SECRET: These aren't jumping beans, but they may seem like it. They can pop open and jump in the pan a bit, so wear an oven mitt when stirring.

CHANGE IT UP: These are great as a salty snack to munch on, but they are also fun as a topper for hummus, cream cheese or other savory dips!

COOKING GLUTEN FREE OR VEGAN? Always read labels to make sure *each* recipe ingredient is gluten free or vegan. Products and ingredient sources can change.

WARM LEMON ROSEMARY OLIVES

PREP TIME: 5 Minutes • **START TO FINISH:** 35 Minutes • **MAKES:** 12 servings (¼ cup)

3 cups mixed olives
2 sprigs fresh rosemary
1 teaspoon crushed red pepper flakes
1 teaspoon grated lemon peel
1 teaspoon olive oil
   Lemon twists, if desired

1 Heat oven to 400°F. On large sheet of foil, place olives, rosemary, pepper flakes and grated lemon peel; drizzle with oil. Fold foil over olive mixture; pinch edges tightly to seal.

2 Bake 30 minutes. Transfer mixture to serving dish. Garnish with lemon twists. Serve warm.

1 Serving Calories 45; Total Fat 4g (Saturated Fat 0.5g, Trans Fat 0g); Cholesterol 0mg; Sodium 250mg; Total Carbohydrate 2g (Dietary Fiber 1g); Protein 0g **Exchanges:** 1 Fat **Carbohydrate Choices:** 0

KITCHEN SECRET: Mixed olives are available in the deli department at most grocery stores.

COOKING GLUTEN FREE? Always read labels to make sure *each* recipe ingredient is gluten free. Products and ingredient sources can change.

MUMBAI CRISPS

PREP TIME: 20 Minutes • **START TO FINISH:** 35 Minutes • **MAKES:** 30 servings (1 chip each)

1 medium russet or Idaho potato, baked, cooled, peeled, cut into ¼-inch cubes (1 cup)

¼ cup diced (¼ inch) red bell pepper

1 tablespoon finely chopped red onion

4 teaspoons chopped fresh cilantro leaves

4 teaspoons chopped fresh mint leaves

1 to 1½ teaspoons finely chopped jalapeño chile

1 tablespoon vegetable oil

1 tablespoon fresh lime juice

¼ teaspoon plus ⅛ teaspoon salt

½ teaspoon ground cumin

30 falafel chips or whole-grain tortilla chips (from 5.5-oz bag)

2 teaspoons finely chopped dry-roasted peanuts

2 teaspoons unsweetened coconut

1 In medium bowl, place potatoes, bell pepper, onion, cilantro, mint and jalapeño. In small bowl, whisk together oil, lime juice, salt and cumin until well mixed. Pour over potato mixture; gently toss to thoroughly coat. Let stand at room temperature 15 minutes to blend flavors.

2 Just before serving, place chips in single layer on very large serving platter. Spoon about 2 teaspoons of the potato mixture onto each chip; sprinkle with peanuts and coconut. Serve immediately.

1 Serving: Calories 25; Total Fat 1.5g (Saturated Fat 0g, Trans Fat 0g); Cholesterol 0mg; Sodium 40mg; Total Carbohydrate 3g (Dietary Fiber 0g); Protein 0g **Exchanges:** 1 Vegetable **Carbohydrate Choices:** 0

KITCHEN SECRET: Unsweetened coconut can be found in the baking aisle or the organic foods section of your grocery store.

TZATZIKI "BRUSCHETTA"

PREP TIME: 20 Minutes • **START TO FINISH:** 20 Minutes • **MAKES:** 4 servings (3 chips each)

12 falafel chips or whole-grain
    tortilla chips (from 5.5-oz bag)
¼ cup plain Greek yogurt
¾ teaspoon fresh lemon juice
    Dash salt
¼ cup diced (¼ inch) English
    (hothouse) cucumber
1 tablespoon chopped fresh
    mint leaves
12 small sprigs fresh dill weed

Arrange chips in single layer on serving platter.
In small bowl, mix yogurt, lemon juice and salt until
well blended. Spoon 1 teaspoon of the yogurt mixture
onto each chip. Top with 1 teaspoon cucumber; sprinkle
with about ¼ teaspoon mint. Top with a dill weed sprig.
Serve immediately.

1 Serving: Calories 20; Total Fat 1g (Saturated Fat 0g, Trans Fat 0g); Cholesterol
0mg; Sodium 25mg; Total Carbohydrate 2g (Dietary Fiber 0g); Protein 0g
Exchanges: 1 Vegetable **Carbohydrate Choices:** 0

KITCHEN SECRET: English (hothouse) or "burpless"
cucumbers have a mild flavor and very few seeds and are
long and thin. Because they are usually not waxed, you
don't need to peel them before use. They're perfect for
this deconstructed tzatziki.

KITCHEN SECRET: We love using fresh lemon juice in
the kitchen, but for convenience, look in your grocery
freezer case for frozen lemon juice, available in plastic
bottles. It's freshly frozen juice. Just thaw and store in the
refrigerator as directed on package.

BUFFALO VEGGIE-STUFFED MUSHROOMS

PREP TIME: 20 Minutes • **START TO FINISH:** 40 Minutes • **MAKES:** About 4 servings (3 mushrooms each)

1 package (8 oz) fresh whole mushrooms

¼ cup frozen riced cauliflower (from 10-oz package)

¼ cup shredded zucchini

2 tablespoons Buffalo wing sauce

⅛ teaspoon gluten-free seasoned salt

2 oz cream cheese (from 8-oz package), softened

2 tablespoons gluten-free blue cheese dressing

1 Heat oven to 375°F.

2 Carefully remove mushroom stems from mushroom caps; place caps stem side up in 15x10-inch pan with sides.

3 Finely chop enough stems to measure ¼ cup. In 1½-quart saucepan, cook chopped mushrooms and all remaining ingredients except cream cheese and dressing over medium heat, stirring frequently, 3 to 4 minutes or until mushrooms are softened. Remove from heat. Stir in cream cheese and dressing until cheese is melted. Fill mushroom caps with mushroom mixture; caps will be very full.

4 Bake 15 to 20 minutes or until thoroughly heated. Serve immediately.

1 Serving: Calories 120; Total Fat 10g (Saturated Fat 4g, Trans Fat 0g); Cholesterol 15mg; Sodium 240mg; Total Carbohydrate 4g (Dietary Fiber 1g); Protein 3g **Exchanges:** 1 Vegetable, 2 Fat **Carbohydrate Choices:** 0

KITCHEN SECRET: After baking, you can top the mushrooms with additional shredded zucchini. Drizzle additional Buffalo wing sauce over the mushrooms, if you like.

KITCHEN SECRET: Each package of mushrooms will vary slightly in number, but usually there are 10 to 14 mushrooms per 8-oz package. Don't worry—we've made sure there is enough filling no matter how many your package holds.

COOKING GLUTEN FREE? Always read labels to make sure *each* recipe ingredient is gluten free. Products and ingredient sources can change.

BLOOMING ONION WITH BACON-CHIPOTLE DIP

PREP TIME: 20 Minutes   •   **START TO FINISH:** 30 Minutes   •   **MAKES:** 8 servings

BACON-CHIPOTLE DIP

- ¼ cup mayonnaise
- 1 to 2 tablespoons chopped canned chipotle chiles in adobo sauce
- 1 tablespoon crumbled cooked bacon

ONION

- ½ cup bite-size squares oven-toasted corn cereal
- ½ cup bite-size squares oven-toasted rice cereal
- ½ cup rice-based gluten-free baking mix
- ¾ teaspoon salt
- ½ teaspoon ground red pepper (cayenne)
- ¼ teaspoon ancho chile powder
- ¼ teaspoon dried thyme leaves
- ¼ teaspoon ground cumin
- ¼ teaspoon black pepper
- ½ cup milk
- 1 egg
- 1 large sweet onion
  Vegetable oil for deep frying

KITCHEN SECRET: To crush cereal, place it in a resealable food-storage plastic bag; seal bag. Finely crush with a rolling pin or meat mallet. Or place in a food processor, cover and process, using quick on-and-off motions, until finely crushed.

① In small bowl, mix Bacon-Chipotle Dip ingredients. Cover and refrigerate until ready to serve.

② Crush cereals. In medium bowl, mix crushed cereals, baking mix, salt and spices. In another medium bowl, beat milk and egg with whisk.

③ Cut ½ inch off pointed end of onion; peel onion, leaving bottom stem. Cut 1-inch diameter core out of middle of onion. Using very sharp large knife, cut through center of onion, about three-fourths of the way down. Rotate onion 90 degrees and cut again across first cut to make X shape. Keep cutting the sections in half, very carefully, until the onion has been cut 16 times. Do not cut down to the bottom of the onion. Spread "petals" of onion apart. Coat onion with cereal mixture, separating petals and sprinkling dry coating between them. Dip onion into egg mixture to coat completely, then dip into cereal mixture to coat. (This double dipping ensures a well-coated onion; some of the coating will fall off when the onion is frying.)

④ In deep fryer or heavy saucepan, place about 3 inches oil, enough to just cover onion. Heat oil to 350°F. Line a plate with paper towels.

⑤ Using slotted spoon, slowly place onion in hot oil. Adjust heat to keep oil at 350°F. Fry 6 to 7 minutes, turning onion with slotted spoon after 3 minutes, until onion is golden brown. Remove with slotted spoon; drain on paper towels. Serve hot with dip.

1 Serving: Calories 320; Total Fat 20g (Saturated Fat 3.5g, Trans Fat 0g); Cholesterol 55mg; Sodium 660mg; Total Carbohydrate 27g (Dietary Fiber 2g); Protein 6g **Exchanges:** 2 Starch, 4 Fat **Carbohydrate Choices:** 2

STEAMED EDAMAME IN THE SHELL WITH DIPPING SAUCES

PREP TIME: 15 Minutes • **START TO FINISH:** 15 Minutes • **MAKES:** 10 servings (10 edamame and 1 tablespoon of each sauce each)

GINGER-SOY DIPPING SAUCE

- ⅔ cup reduced-sodium or regular soy sauce
- 2 tablespoons honey
- 2 teaspoons finely chopped fresh gingerroot
- ½ teaspoon crushed red pepper flakes
- 2 thinly sliced green onions (2 tablespoons)

CREAMY WASABI DIPPING SAUCE

- ½ cup mayonnaise
- ⅓ cup sour cream
- 2 teaspoons wasabi powder
- ¼ teaspoon salt

EDAMAME

- 1 bag (12 oz) frozen edamame soybeans (in the pod)

1 In small bowl, mix all Ginger-Soy Dipping Sauce ingredients, except onions, until well blended; stir in onions. In another small bowl, mix Creamy Wasabi Dipping Sauce ingredients until smooth. Set sauces aside.

2 In 4-quart saucepan, place steamer basket. Pour in 1 cup water; heat to boiling. Place edamame in basket; cover and steam 3 to 6 minutes or until crisp-tender.

3 Using slotted spoon, transfer edamame from basket to serving bowl. Let stand until cool enough to handle. Serve warm or room temperature with Dipping Sauces.

1 Serving: Calories 150; Total Fat 11g (Saturated Fat 2.5g, Trans Fat 0g); Cholesterol 10mg; Sodium 710mg; Total Carbohydrate 8g (Dietary Fiber 1g); Protein 3g **Exchanges:** ½ Other Carbohydrate, ½ Vegetable, 2 Fat **Carbohydrate Choices:** ½

KITCHEN SECRET: Wasabi, also called Japanese horseradish, has a sharp, pungent, fiery flavor. It comes in both powder and paste forms and is available in the Asian aisle of large supermarkets. If you can't find it, drained regular prepared horseradish makes a great substitute. An easy garnish for this sauce is a sprinkling of black sesame seed.

KITCHEN SECRET: Fresh edamame (green soybeans), found in the produce section, can be substituted for frozen edamame. Increase steaming time to 20 minutes.

SUN-DRIED TOMATO AND BASIL YOGURT BARK

PREP TIME: 15 Minutes　•　**START TO FINISH:** 3 Hours 15 Minutes　•　**MAKES:** 12 pieces

- 1½ cups plain whole milk (5%) Greek yogurt
- ¼ cup grated Parmesan cheese
- 2 oz cream cheese (from 8-oz package), softened
- ¼ cup plus 2 tablespoons chopped drained sun-dried tomatoes packed in oil
- 3 tablespoons chopped fresh basil leaves
- 1 tablespoon toasted pine nuts
- 2 teaspoons balsamic glaze

1 Line 9-inch square pan with foil, letting foil hang over two opposite sides of pan.

2 In medium bowl, beat yogurt, Parmesan cheese and cream cheese with spoon until well mixed. Stir in ¼ cup of the sun-dried tomatoes and 2 tablespoons of the basil; spread mixture evenly in bottom of pan. Top with remaining 2 tablespoons sun-dried tomatoes and remaining 1 tablespoon basil; sprinkle with pine nuts. With fork, drizzle top with balsamic glaze.

3 Cover pan with foil and freeze at least 3 hours or until yogurt mixture is hard.

4 Transfer bark from pan to cutting board by lifting foil; remove and discard foil. Let stand 3 minutes before cutting. With sharp knife, cut into 4 rows by 3 rows. Serve immediately.

1 Piece: Calories 70; Total Fat 4.5g (Saturated Fat 2g, Trans Fat 0g); Cholesterol 10mg; Sodium 65mg; Total Carbohydrate 3g (Dietary Fiber 0g); Protein 4g **Exchanges:** ½ High-Fat Meat **Carbohydrate Choices:** 0

CHANGE IT UP: Start the weekend off with this savory new and interesting take on yogurt bark. Serve with a toasted gluten-free baguette and a cocktail or a glass of wine!

HOW TO STORE: Store leftovers in an airtight container in the freezer up to 3 days.

KITCHEN SECRET: Balsamic glaze is basically a reduced form of balsamic vinegar. Also known as balsamic reduction, it provides notes of sour and sweet and pairs nicely with the sun-dried tomato and basil in this yogurt bark. You can pour small amounts on a fork and gently shake it over the bark to drizzle. Or for even more control in drizzling, transfer to a resealable food-storage plastic bag; seal bag. Cut off a tiny corner of the bag; drizzle glaze on top of bark.

COOKING GLUTEN FREE? Always read labels to make sure *each* recipe ingredient is gluten free. Products and ingredient sources can change.

PARSLEY DEVILED EGGS

PREP TIME: 20 Minutes • **START TO FINISH:** 25 Minutes • **MAKES:** 8 servings (2 egg halves each)

8 hard-cooked eggs

¼ cup mayonnaise or gluten-free salad dressing

2 tablespoons chopped fresh parsley leaves

½ teaspoon ground mustard

¼ teaspoon salt

¼ teaspoon pepper

1. Peel eggs; cut lengthwise in half. Slip out yolks into small bowl; mash with fork. Stir in remaining ingredients.

2. Fill whites with egg yolk mixture, heaping lightly. Arrange eggs on serving plate. Serve immediately or cover and refrigerate up to 24 hours.

1 Serving: Calories 120; Total Fat 11g (Saturated Fat 2.5g, Trans Fat 0g); Cholesterol 190mg; Sodium 180mg; Total Carbohydrate 0g (Dietary Fiber 0g); Protein 6g **Exchanges:** 1 Medium-Fat Meat, 1 Fat **Carbohydrate Choices:** 0

KITCHEN SECRET: It's easy to make hard-cooked eggs just right! Place eggs in a saucepan and cover with cold water. Heat to boiling, then remove from the heat. Cover and let stand 15 minutes. Immediately cool briefly in cold water to prevent further cooking. Tap an egg to crack shell; roll the egg between your hands to loosen the shell, then peel.

KITCHEN SECRET: For an interesting, elegant look, cut eggs in half with a waffle-fry cutter.

COOKING GLUTEN FREE? Always read labels to make sure *each* recipe ingredient is gluten free. Products and ingredient sources can change.

FRESH DILL YOGURT DIP

PREP TIME: 20 Minutes • **START TO FINISH:** 20 Minutes • **MAKES:** 4 servings (3 tablespoons dip and ½ cup veggies each)

1 container (6 oz) plain fat-free Greek yogurt

3 tablespoons diced red bell pepper

2 tablespoons thinly sliced green onions (2 medium)

1 tablespoon chopped fresh or 1 teaspoon dried dill weed

¼ teaspoon salt

Dash ground red pepper (cayenne)

1 small clove garlic, minced

½ cup ready-to-eat baby-cut carrots

1 cup broccoli florets

½ medium cucumber, thinly sliced (1 cup)

In small bowl, mix yogurt, bell pepper, green onions, dill weed, salt, red pepper and garlic until well blended. Serve with carrots, broccoli and cucumber slices.

1 Serving: Calories 50; Total Fat 0g (Saturated Fat 0g, Trans Fat 0g); Cholesterol 0mg; Sodium 180mg; Total Carbohydrate 6g (Dietary Fiber 1g); Protein 5g **Exchanges:** ½ Starch, ½ Very Lean Meat **Carbohydrate Choices:** ½

KITCHEN SECRET: Cut up the veggies in advance and store in resealable food-storage plastic bags in the refrigerator. The dip can be made the day before it's served; just cover and refrigerate.

CHANGE IT UP: Serve any of your favorite fresh vegetables with this dip. Try green bell peppers, celery, cauliflower or grape tomatoes.

KITCHEN SECRET: If you like, sprinkle the dip with an additional 2 tablespoons chopped red bell pepper before serving.

COOKING GLUTEN FREE? Always read labels to make sure *each* recipe ingredient is gluten free. Products and ingredient sources can change.

BASIL-SPINACH DIP

PREP TIME: 15 Minutes   •   **START TO FINISH:** 15 Minutes   •   **MAKES:** 16 servings (3 tablespoons each)

- 1 box (9 oz) frozen chopped spinach
- 1½ cups plain fat-free yogurt
- ¾ cup reduced-fat mayonnaise or salad dressing
- ¼ cup chopped fresh or 1 tablespoon dried basil leaves
- 2 tablespoons chopped green onions (2 medium)
- ½ teaspoon garlic salt
- 1 can (8 oz) water chestnuts, drained, chopped

1. Cook spinach as directed on package. Cool slightly; squeeze to drain well.

2. In large bowl, mix all ingredients. Chill before serving.

1 Serving: Calories 60; Total Fat 4g (Saturated Fat 0.5g, Trans Fat 0g); Cholesterol 0mg; Sodium 135mg; Total Carbohydrate 5g (Dietary Fiber 0g); Protein 1g **Exchanges:** ½ Other Carbohydrate, 1 Fat **Carbohydrate Choices:** ½

KITCHEN SECRET: Vegetables marry well with this herb dip. Include baby carrots, radishes, sugar snap peas, sliced cucumber or halved grape and/or cherry tomatoes in your array.

CHANGE IT UP: Sliced green onion is an easy garnish, or pepper it up with chopped red bell pepper and serve it with additional slices of red pepper for dipping.

COOKING GLUTEN FREE? Always read labels to make sure *each* recipe ingredient is gluten free. Products and ingredient sources can change.

SPICY SPINACH AND ARTICHOKE DIP

PREP TIME: 15 Minutes • **START TO FINISH:** 40 Minutes • **MAKES:** 16 servings

1 box (9 oz) frozen spinach, thawed, squeezed to drain

1 can (13.75 oz) artichoke hearts, drained, chopped

1 clove garlic, finely chopped

¼ cup sliced green onions (4 medium)

¼ cup chopped red bell pepper

1 cup sour cream

½ cup mayonnaise or salad dressing

½ cup grated Parmesan cheese

1½ cups shredded pepper Jack cheese (6 oz)

12 oz pita chips (about 96 chips)

1 Heat oven to 350°F.

2 In large bowl, mix all ingredients except pita chips. Spoon into ungreased 9- or 10-inch glass pie plate.

3 Bake 20 to 25 minutes or until thoroughly heated. Serve hot with pita chips.

1 Serving: Calories 240; Total Fat 16g (Saturated Fat 5g, Trans Fat 0g); Cholesterol 25mg; Sodium 400mg; Total Carbohydrate 19g (Dietary Fiber 2g); Protein 7g **Exchanges:** 1 Starch, ½ Other Carbohydrate, ½ Medium-Fat Meat, 2½ Fat **Carbohydrate Choices:** 1

CHANGE IT UP: Serve with slices of baguette or garlic toast instead of pita chips for a yummy twist.

BEER CHEESE DIP

PREP TIME: 20 Minutes • **START TO FINISH:** 20 Minutes • **MAKES:** 16 servings (about ¼ cup dip each)

1 clove garlic, cut in half
¼ cup butter
¼ cup all-purpose flour
1 can or bottle (12 oz) regular or nonalcoholic beer
6 cups shredded mild cheddar cheese (1½ lb)

1 Rub inside of 3-quart saucepan with cut sides of garlic; discard garlic. Place butter in saucepan; melt over low heat. Stir in flour with whisk; cook 2 minutes, stirring constantly. Stir in beer. Increase heat to medium-high; heat to boiling. Boil 2 to 3 minutes, stirring constantly, until mixture is thick and smooth.

2 Reduce heat to low. Add cheese about ½ cup at a time, stirring until cheese is melted and mixture is smooth before adding next ½ cup.

3 Transfer dip to fondue pot; immediately place fondue pot over flame. Serve with dippers.

1 Serving: Calories 210; Total Fat 17g (Saturated Fat 10g, Trans Fat 0.5g); Cholesterol 50mg; Sodium 300mg; Total Carbohydrate 3g (Dietary Fiber 0g); Protein 10g **Exchanges:** 1½ High-Fat Meat, 1 Fat **Carbohydrate Choices:** 0

CHANGE IT UP: If you like your dip spicy, stir ¼ to ½ teaspoon red pepper sauce into the cheese sauce once it is melted and smooth.

CHANGE IT UP: If you don't have a fondue pot, keep the dip warm in a 1½-quart slow cooker.

KITCHEN SECRET: Sprinkle dip with chopped green onion for a simple garnish.

KITCHEN SECRET: You can always serve veggies with this dip, but expand the possibilities with assorted dippers like rye or sourdough bread cubes, ham or turkey cubes, apple or pear wedges, pretzel twists or nuggets, soft pretzels, smoked cocktail sausages or sliced fully cooked Polish sausage.

SPICY INDIAN MOZZARELLA BITES WITH CURRY AIOLI

PREP TIME: 20 Minutes • **START TO FINISH:** 30 Minutes • **MAKES:** 6 servings (4 bites and 1 tablespoon aioli each)

CURRY AIOLI

- ⅓ cup mayonnaise
- 1 teaspoon curry powder
- ⅛ teaspoon red pepper sauce

MOZZARELLA BITES

- 1 container (8 oz) 1-inch fresh mozzarella cheese balls (ciliegine)
- ¼ cup all-purpose flour
- 1 egg
- 1 teaspoon water
- ½ cup plain panko crispy bread crumbs
- 2 tablespoons chopped fresh parsley
- 2 teaspoons garam masala
- ¼ teaspoon salt
- Cooking spray

1 In small bowl, stir together all Curry Aioli ingredients; cover and refrigerate until ready to serve.

2 Drain mozzarella balls; pat dry with paper towels. Place flour in shallow bowl. In another shallow bowl, lightly beat egg and water to mix. In third shallow bowl, mix bread crumbs, parsley, garam masala and salt.

3 Set oven control to broil. Line cookie sheet with foil.

4 Roll each cheese ball in flour; tap off any excess flour. Coat in egg mixture, then roll in bread crumb mixture. Place balls in cookie sheet at least 1 inch apart. Spray balls with cooking spray.

5 Broil with tops of cheese balls about 7 inches from heat 2 to 4 minutes or just until golden brown. (Watch carefully so cheese does not burn.) Let cool 5 minutes.

6 Serve with Curry Aioli.

1 Serving: Calories 270; Total Fat 20g (Saturated Fat 8g, Trans Fat 0g); Cholesterol 70mg; Sodium 480mg; Total Carbohydrate 12g (Dietary Fiber 0g); Protein 11g **Exchanges:** ½ Other Carbohydrate, ½ Low-Fat Milk, 1 Medium-Fat Meat, 2½ Fat **Carbohydrate Choices:** 1

CHANGE IT UP: The Curry Aioli is also terrific as a sandwich spread, as a dip for vegetables or as an accompaniment for sliced ham. If you like, you can also skip the Curry Aioli and serve the mozzarella bites with marinara sauce or chutney.

KITCHEN SECRET: These breaded cheese balls require careful attention when under the broiler. You want to broil them just long enough to get golden brown but not so long that they burn or lose their shape.

CHANGE IT UP: Sprinkle with chopped parsley if you like a bit more color.

WHITE BEAN HUMMUS-FILLED VEGETABLES WITH GREMOLATA

PREP TIME: 20 Minutes • **START TO FINISH:** 35 Minutes • **MAKES:** 4 servings

VEGGIES AND HUMMUS

- 4 mini bell peppers (red, yellow and orange)
- 2 fresh Campari tomatoes
- ¼ large English (hothouse) cucumber
- 10 tablespoons white bean hummus, stirred to blend (from 10-oz container)

GREMOLATA

- 2 tablespoons pine nuts, coarsely chopped
- 1 tablespoon freshly grated-free Parmesan cheese
- 1 tablespoon finely chopped fresh Italian (flat-leaf) parsley
- ½ teaspoon finely shredded lemon zest
- ½ teaspoon fresh lemon juice
- ½ teaspoon finely chopped garlic
- ½ teaspoon olive oil
- ⅛ teaspoon fine sea salt

1 Cut mini bell peppers in half lengthwise; scoop out any seeds and membranes with a teaspoon. Quarter tomatoes and scoop out flesh. Using vegetable peeler, cut 4 lengthwise strips from cucumber peel to make striped pattern. Cut cucumber into ½-inch-thick rounds. Using teaspoon or melon baller, scoop out center of each cucumber round, taking care not to cut all the way through. Set vegetables aside.

2 Place hummus into 1-quart resealable food-storage plastic bag; seal bag. Cut off small corner of bag; squeeze hummus from bag to fill vegetables. Place filled vegetables on platter.

3 In small bowl, mix all Gremolata ingredients. Top vegetables with Gremolata and serve.

1 Serving: Calories 180; Total Fat 8g (Saturated Fat 1g, Trans Fat 0g); Cholesterol 0mg; Sodium 270mg; Total Carbohydrate 21g (Dietary Fiber 6g); Protein 6g **Exchanges:** ½ Starch, 2½ Vegetable, 1½ Fat **Carbohydrate Choices:** 1½

KITCHEN SECRET: Campari tomatoes are larger than cherry tomatoes (about the size of a golf ball) and are readily available. If you don't have Campari tomatoes, you can substitute plum (Roma) tomatoes.

CHANGE IT UP: Don't have pine nuts? Substitute slivered almonds in the Gremolata for a slightly different flavor.

COOKING GLUTEN FREE? Always read labels to make sure *each* recipe ingredient is gluten free. Products and ingredient sources can change.

SMOKED SALMON SPREAD

PREP TIME: 20 Minutes • **START TO FINISH:** 1 Hour 20 Minutes • **MAKES:** 24 servings
(2 tablespoons spread and 4 crackers each)

2 packages (8 oz each) cream
  cheese, softened

1 container (8 oz) sour cream

2 tablespoons chopped fresh
  dill weed

1 teaspoon lemon-
  pepper seasoning

4 oz smoked salmon, flaked

½ cup finely chopped red
  bell pepper

96 crackers

1 Line 3-cup bowl or pan with plastic wrap, letting plastic wrap hang over edge. In large bowl, stir together cream cheese, ½ cup of the sour cream, dill weed and lemon-pepper seasoning until well blended.

2 Spoon half of the cream cheese mixture by heaping tablespoonfuls into bowl; spread and press to cover bottom of bowl. Top evenly with salmon. Spoon remaining cheese mixture by tablespoonfuls over salmon; spread to cover salmon layer. Fold plastic wrap over top of cheese to cover completely; press lightly to compact cheese and salmon. Refrigerate 1 hour.

3 Remove plastic wrap from top of cheese mixture. Place serving plate upside down on bowl; turn plate and bowl over together. Remove bowl, then plastic wrap. Using rubber spatula, spread remaining ½ cup sour cream over cheese mixture. Sprinkle bell pepper over sour cream. Serve with crackers.

1 Serving: Calories 160; Total Fat 12g (Saturated Fat 5g, Trans Fat 0g); Cholesterol 25mg; Sodium 200mg; Total Carbohydrate 10g (Dietary Fiber 0g); Protein 3g **Exchanges:** ½ Other Carbohydrate, ½ Medium-Fat Meat, 2 Fat **Carbohydrate Choices:** ½

CHANGE IT UP: For added color, garnish with dill weed sprigs or fresh parsley. Don't have fresh dill weed available? Use 2 teaspoons dried dill weed instead.

SLOW-COOKER BACON CHEESEBURGER DIP

PREP TIME: 20 Minutes • **START TO FINISH:** 2 Hours 20 Minutes • **MAKES:** 28 servings
(2 tablespoons dip, 2 bell pepper strips and 1 bagel chip each)

8 slices bacon

½ lb ground beef (at least 80% lean)

1 package (8 oz) cream cheese, cut into cubes

1 package (8 oz) shredded American-cheddar cheese blend (2 cups)

1 can (10 oz) diced tomatoes with green chiles, undrained

2 tablespoons chopped fresh parsley leaves

2 medium red bell peppers, cut into bite-size strips

1 package (5.25 oz) mini bagel chips

1 In 12-inch skillet, cook bacon over medium-high heat, turning occasionally, until crisp; drain on paper towels. Crumble bacon; reserve 2 tablespoons for garnish.

2 In same skillet, cook beef over medium-high heat 5 to 7 minutes, stirring occasionally, until thoroughly cooked; drain. Reduce heat to low. Add cheeses, tomatoes and crumbled bacon; stir until well mixed and cheeses start to melt.

3 Spray 1- to 1½-quart slow cooker with cooking spray. Spoon or pour bacon cheeseburger mixture into slow cooker. Cover; cook on Low heat setting 2 to 3 hours or until hot and bubbly.

4 Stir parsley into dip. Sprinkle with reserved bacon. Keep on Low heat setting to serve. Serve with bell pepper strips and bagel chips.

1 Serving: Calories 110; Total Fat 8g (Saturated Fat 4g, Trans Fat 0g); Cholesterol 25mg; Sodium 150mg; Total Carbohydrate 5g (Dietary Fiber 0g); Protein 5g **Exchanges:** ½ Other Carbohydrate, ½ High-Fat Meat, 1 Fat **Carbohydrate Choices:** ½

KITCHEN SECRET: You can microwave bacon quickly and eliminate the spattering that happens when it's cooked on the stove: Place bacon on a microwavable plate lined with paper towels. Place paper towels between layers; cover with a paper towel. Eight slices will take 4 to 6 minutes on High.

KITCHEN SECRET: Just like bagels, bagel chips come in a wide variety of flavors. We call for mini bagel chips, but regular-size chips work well, too. Any savory chip goes well with this cheesy dip: plain, rye, garlic or everything.

GLUTEN FREE　**VEGETARIAN**　**PARTY READY**

TEX-MEX TAILGATE DIP

PREP TIME: 20 Minutes　•　**START TO FINISH:** 20 Minutes　•　**MAKES:** 16 servings (½ cup each)

1　can (16 oz) vegetarian refried beans

1　package (1 oz) gluten-free taco seasoning mix

1　package (8 oz) gluten-free cream cheese, softened

1　can (4.5 oz) chopped green chiles

1　cup chunky salsa (any variety)

2　cups shredded lettuce

2　cups shredded cheddar cheese or gluten-free Mexican cheese blend (8 oz)

1　can (2.25 oz) sliced ripe olives, drained (½ cup)

1　medium tomato, diced (¾ cup)

1　In medium bowl, mix refried beans and taco seasoning mix. Spread mixture on large platter.

2　In another medium bowl, mix cream cheese and chiles. Carefully spread over bean mixture.

3　Top with salsa, lettuce, cheddar cheese, olives and tomato. Refrigerate until serving time.

1 Serving: Calories 160; Total Fat 11g (Saturated Fat 6g, Trans Fat 0g); Cholesterol 30mg; Sodium 550mg; Total Carbohydrate 9g (Dietary Fiber 2g); Protein 6g **Exchanges:** ½ Other Carbohydrate, 1 High-Fat Meat, ½ Fat **Carbohydrate Choices:** ½

KITCHEN SECRET: For an eighth layer to this dip—and extra creamy goodness—sprinkle chopped ripe avocado on top of the bean mixture, before the cheese. Top with fresh cilantro sprigs.

KITCHEN SECRET: Serve this dip with your favorite gluten-free tortilla chips, or make crisp veggie "chips" with sliced zucchini, carrot coins, jicama slices or sticks and bell pepper strips.

COOKING GLUTEN FREE? Always read labels to make sure *each* recipe ingredient is gluten free. Products and ingredient sources can change.

TOASTED ROSEMARY NUTS

PREP TIME: 15 Minutes • **START TO FINISH:** 1 Hour 20 Minutes • **MAKES:** 12 servings (¼ cup each)

2 tablespoons finely chopped fresh rosemary leaves

1 tablespoon butter, melted

1 teaspoon organic sugar

1 teaspoon salt

¼ teaspoon ground red pepper (cayenne)

3 cups raw nuts (almonds, pecans, cashews)

1 Heat oven to 300°F. Spray 18x13-inch half-sheet pan with cooking spray.

2 In medium bowl, mix rosemary, butter, sugar, salt and red pepper. Add nuts; stir to coat.

3 Spread nuts on pan in even layer. Bake 30 to 35 minutes, stirring after about 15 minutes, until nuts are toasted. Cool completely, about 30 minutes.

1 Serving: Calories 230; Total Fat 19g (Saturated Fat 2g, Trans Fat 0g); Cholesterol 0mg; Sodium 200mg; Total Carbohydrate 8g (Dietary Fiber 4g); Protein 7g **Exchanges:** ½ Other Carbohydrate, 1 High-Fat Meat, 2 Fat **Carbohydrate Choices:** ½

CHANGE IT UP: You can use any nut you like in the recipe. Pick one or use several for a mixed nut snack.

HOW TO STORE: Store in an airtight container at room temperature up to 5 days.

COOKING GLUTEN FREE? Always read labels to make sure *each* recipe ingredient is gluten free. Products and ingredient sources can change.

20 MINUTES OR LESS

SWEET

GALACTIC FRO-YO BARK

PREP TIME: 20 Minutes • **START TO FINISH:** 5 Hours 20 Minutes • **MAKES:** 12 pieces

12 tubes (6 of each flavor, 2 oz each) berry yogurt and strawberry yogurt (from 16-count box or two 8-count boxes)

1¼ teaspoons blue gel food color

2 tablespoons cookie cereal

1 tablespoon O-shaped honey-nut cereal

2 tablespoons fresh blueberries (about 10 blueberries)

4 fresh blackberries, halved crosswise

Assorted star candy sprinkles, gold and silver nonpareils

1. Line large cookie sheet with cooking parchment paper.

2. Squeeze berry yogurt tubes into small bowl; stir to mix. Squeeze 3 strawberry yogurt tubes into each of 2 small bowls. Add 1 teaspoon food color to one of the strawberry yogurt bowls and ¼ teaspoon food color to other. Stir each with separate spoons, leaving some streaks of deeper blue in each.

3. Drop spoonfuls of each yogurt onto cookie sheet in random pattern within 12×10-inch area. Using tip of offset metal spatula or spoon, carefully swirl yogurt colors to look like a galaxy. Carefully skim across top of yogurt mixture using edge of offset metal spatula to create flat, even layer about ¼ inch thick. Top evenly with cereals, berries and sprinkles. Freeze uncovered 30 minutes.

4. Loosely cover with foil. Return to freezer 4½ to 5½ hours or until firmly set.

5. Break apart into 12 equal-size pieces and serve immediately.

1 Piece: Calories 90; Total Fat 2.5g (Saturated Fat 1g, Trans Fat 0g); Cholesterol 5mg; Sodium 30mg; Total Carbohydrate 15g (Dietary Fiber 0g); Protein 2g **Exchanges:** 1 Starch, ½ Fat **Carbohydrate Choices:** 1

KITCHEN SECRET: Yogurt bark starts to melt quickly, so be sure to keep it in the freezer until just before serving.

KITCHEN SECRET: Stirring yogurt before spooning it onto cookie sheet will help eliminate any lumps.

HOW TO STORE: Store in a covered container in the freezer up to 1 week.

CHERRY-KEY LIME PIE POPS

PREP TIME: 20 Minutes • **START TO FINISH:** 8 Hours 20 Minutes • **MAKES:** 12 pops

- ¼ cup graham cracker crumbs
- 1 tablespoon butter, melted
- 1 package (8 oz) cream cheese, softened
- 1 can (14 oz) sweetened condensed milk
- ¾ cup bottled Key lime juice
- 3 drops green liquid food color
- 1 container (8 oz) frozen whipped topping, thawed
- 1 cup cherry pie filling (from 21-oz can)
- 12 craft sticks

KITCHEN SECRET: Cutting the cherries slightly helps the pie filling swirl more easily with the Key lime mixture. Using a kitchen scissors to cut the cherries in the measuring cup keeps your fingers clean and eliminates the mess of a knife and cutting board.

HOW TO STORE: If you won't be eating all the pops right away, wrap them individually with plastic wrap and store in the freezer up to 1 week for easy snacking.

CHANGE IT UP: Berry instead of cherry? Substitute raspberry pie filling for the cherry pie filling.

1. Line 9x5-inch loaf pan with heavy-duty foil, letting foil hang over two opposite sides of pan.

2. In small bowl, stir graham cracker crumbs and butter until well mixed. Spread over bottom of loaf pan.

3. In large bowl, using electric mixer, beat cream cheese on medium speed until smooth. Add condensed milk; beat until smooth. Beat in lime juice and food color; beat until blended. Fold in whipped topping. Spoon half of the lime mixture over crumbs in pan.

4. With kitchen scissors, cut cherries in pie filling into smaller pieces; spoon pie filling over lime mixture in pan. Spoon remaining lime mixture over cherries. With metal spatula, swirl top lime mixture through cherry layer. Cover with heavy-duty foil over top of pan; seal edges.

5. Make 2 rows of 6 tiny cuts in foil with sharp knife. Place a craft stick through each cut into pop layers, leaving 1½ inches of stick visible. Freeze for at least 8 hours or until firm.

6. Remove foil from top of pan. Transfer from pan to cutting board by lifting lining foil; pull back foil from sides. Cut pop mixture in half lengthwise, then cut crosswise between sticks to make 12 pops. Return to freezer until ready to serve.

1 Pop: Calories 280; Total Fat 15g (Saturated Fat 10g, Trans Fat 0g); Cholesterol 35mg; Sodium 130mg; Total Carbohydrate 31g (Dietary Fiber 0g); Protein 4g **Exchanges:** 2 Other Carbohydrate, ½ High-Fat Meat, 2 Fat **Carbohydrate Choices:** 2

20 Minutes or Less **Sweet**

FRUITY PRETZEL CRAYONS

PREP TIME: 20 Minutes • **START TO FINISH:** 20 Minutes • **MAKES:** 4 servings (2 crayons each)

4 pretzel rods
4 chewy fruit-flavored snacks in various colors (red, blue, green, yellow)

1. Line small platter with cooking parchment paper.

2. Cut pretzel rods in half with serrated knife.

3. Unroll and remove paper from fruit flavored snacks. Cut each into 4 (1½-inch-wide) strips.

4. Wrap 1 strip around each pretzel rod half, covering entire pretzel, and pressing gently to attach. Form one end of strip around pretzel to make the crayon tip.

5. Cut thin strips about 2 inches long and ¼ inch wide, using another color fruit flavored snack. Wrap strip around pretzel rod, near the end, using photo as a guide. Place completed crayons on platter.

1 Serving: Calories 90; Total Fat 1.5g (Saturated Fat 0g, Trans Fat 0g); Cholesterol 0mg; Sodium 150mg; Total Carbohydrate 19g (Dietary Fiber 0g); Protein 1g **Exchanges:** 1 Other Carbohydrate, ½ Fat **Carbohydrate Choices:** 1

KITCHEN SECRET: Make up a few of each color to create your own "box" of crayons. This would also make a fun sorting activity, with an edible treat at the end!

CHANGE IT UP: Want to make mini crayons? Instead of pretzel rods, use whole pretzel sticks, and adjust the proportions of fruit-flavored snacks.

MOJITO MELON KABOBS

PREP TIME: 20 Minutes • **START TO FINISH:** 1 Hour 20 Minutes • **MAKES:** 6 kabobs

1 large lime
  About 2½ cups 1-inch cubes assorted melons (¾ lb)
3 tablespoons sugar
2 tablespoons dark rum, if desired
1½ tablespoons finely chopped fresh mint leaves
6 (5- or 6-inch) bamboo skewers

1 Grate 1 tablespoon zest from the lime. Cut lime in half crosswise; squeeze halves into small bowl to get 3 tablespoons juice.

2 Place melon cubes in 1-gallon resealable food-storage plastic bag. Sprinkle with lime zest and pour lime juice over melon. Add sugar, rum if using and mint. Seal bag; turn to coat melon.

3 Refrigerate at least 1 hour to blend flavors but no longer than 24 hours. To serve, thread 4 or 5 melon cubes on each skewer. Discard marinade.

1 Kabob: Calories 50; Total Fat 0g (Saturated Fat 0g, Trans Fat 0g); Cholesterol 0mg; Sodium 10mg; Total Carbohydrate 13g (Dietary Fiber 1g); Protein 0g **Exchanges:** 1 Other Carbohydrate **Carbohydrate Choices:** 1

KITCHEN SECRET: "Mojito" typically refers to a cocktail made with fresh lime juice, sugar, mint leaves and rum. We've taken those same flavors and turned them into a refreshing kabob.

CHANGE IT UP: You can substitute 3 tablespoons frozen limeade concentrate, thawed, for the rum.

COOKING GLUTEN FREE OR VEGAN? Always read labels to make sure *each* recipe ingredient is gluten free or vegan. Products and ingredient sources can change.

SPICED PUMPKIN, APPLE AND JALAPEÑO DIP

PREP TIME: 15 Minutes • **START TO FINISH:** 15 Minutes • **MAKES:** 16 servings (2 tablespoons each)

1 medium jalapeño chile, chopped

4 oz (half of 8-oz package) cream cheese, softened

¼ cup packed organic brown sugar

1 cup canned pumpkin (from 15-oz can; not pumpkin pie mix)

1 medium apple, peeled and shredded (about 1 cup)

2 tablespoons roasted salted hulled pumpkin seeds (pepitas)

1 teaspoon pumpkin pie spice

1 Reserve 1 teaspoon chopped chile for garnish. Finely chop remaining chopped chile.

2 In medium bowl, beat cream cheese and sugar with spoon until well blended. Stir in pumpkin, apple, 1 tablespoon of the pumpkin seeds, the pumpkin pie spice and chopped jalapeño until well mixed.

3 Spoon into serving bowl; sprinkle with remaining 1 tablespoon pumpkin seeds and reserved jalapeño slices. Serve immediately or cover and refrigerate up to 24 hours.

1 Serving: Calories 60; Total Fat 3g (Saturated Fat 1.5g, Trans Fat 0g); Cholesterol 5mg; Sodium 25mg; Total Carbohydrate 6g (Dietary Fiber 0g); Protein 1g **Exchanges:** ½ Starch, ½ Fat **Carbohydrate Choices:** ½

KITCHEN SECRET: Can't decide whether to go sweet or savory with your dippers? Try both. Serve with gluten-free graham crackers, vanilla wafers or thin ginger cookies to keep things sweet. For savory flavors, offer gluten-free seeded crackers or crostini, or veggies such as carrots, celery or fresh sugar snap peas.

CHANGE IT UP: Swap out the apple and use a shredded ripe pear. To add smoky spice, stir in ¼ teaspoon ground chipotle chile pepper.

COOKING GLUTEN FREE? Always read labels to make sure *each* recipe ingredient is gluten free. Products and ingredient sources can change.

GLUTEN FREE **VEGETARIAN** **PARTY READY**

STRAWBERRY-MARSHMALLOW FRUIT DIP

PREP TIME: 15 Minutes • **START TO FINISH:** 1 Hour 15 Minutes • **MAKES:** 15 servings
(2 tablespoons dip and 6 pieces fruit each)

4 oz (half of 8-oz package) gluten-free ⅓-less-fat cream cheese (Neufchâtel), softened

1 cup marshmallow creme (from 7-oz jar)

1 container (6 oz) vegetarian strawberry fat-free Greek yogurt

½ cup chopped fresh strawberries

15 whole fresh strawberries, cut lengthwise in half

30 pieces cut-up melon

30 seedless grapes

1 In medium bowl, beat cream cheese, marshmallow creme, yogurt and chopped strawberries with electric mixer on high speed until smooth. Cover; refrigerate at least 1 hour.

2 Serve dip with whole strawberries, melon, and grapes.

1 Serving: Calories 70; Total Fat 2g (Saturated Fat 1g, Trans Fat 0g); Cholesterol 5mg; Sodium 40mg; Total Carbohydrate 12g (Dietary Fiber 0g); Protein 2g **Exchanges:** ½ Fruit, ½ Other Carbohydrate, ½ Fat **Carbohydrate Choices:** 1

KITCHEN SECRET: You can make the dip up to a day ahead; cover and refrigerate. Stir before serving.

CHANGE IT UP: Use sugar wafers, chocolate wafer cookies or fudge-striped shortbread cookies as dippers as well as fruit for a crunchy, fun change of pace.

COOKING GLUTEN FREE? Always read labels to make sure *each* recipe ingredient is gluten free. Products and ingredient sources can change.

CHURRO RANGOONS WITH SPICY CHOCOLATE SAUCE

PREP TIME: 20 Minutes • **START TO FINISH:** 20 Minutes • **MAKES:** 4 servings (3 rangoons and 2 tablespoons sauce each)

SAUCE
- ⅓ cup heavy whipping cream
- ¼ cup semisweet chocolate chips
- ¼ teaspoon ground cinnamon
- ¼ teaspoon ground chipotle chile pepper

CHURRO RANGOONS
- 2 tablespoons granulated sugar
- ¼ teaspoon plus ⅛ teaspoon ground cinnamon
- ⅓ cup cream cheese spread (from 8-oz container)
- 1 tablespoon packed brown sugar
- 12 (about 3¼-inch) square wonton wraps (from 12-oz package)
- ¼ cup finely chopped pecans
- 1 tablespoon butter

1 In 1-quart saucepan, heat whipping cream over low heat until hot (do not boil); remove from heat. Stir in remaining Sauce ingredients until chocolate is melted; pour into serving bowl and set aside.

2 In small bowl, mix granulated sugar and ¼ teaspoon cinnamon; set aside.

3 In small bowl, mix cream cheese spread, brown sugar and ⅛ teaspoon cinnamon. Spread a teaspoon of cream cheese mixture over each wonton wrap; sprinkle with 1 teaspoon of the pecans. Roll up. Repeat with remaining cream cheese mixture, wonton wraps, and pecans.

4 In 12-inch nonstick skillet, heat butter over medium-high heat until melted. Cook rolls in butter, seam side down, 1 to 2 minutes, turning occasionally, until golden brown. Transfer to paper towels to drain.

5 Sprinkle sugar-cinnamon mixture over hot rolls. Serve with chocolate sauce.

1 Serving: Calories 380; Total Fat 25g (Saturated Fat 12g, Trans Fat 0.5g); Cholesterol 50mg; Sodium 130mg; Total Carbohydrate 34g (Dietary Fiber 2g); Protein 5g **Exchanges:** ½ Starch, 2 Other Carbohydrate, ½ High-Fat Meat, 4 Fat **Carbohydrate Choices:** 2

KITCHEN SECRET: The right temperature of the skillet is the key to success for these cream cheese–filled rolls. When it's hot enough, the rolls won't get soggy from the butter, but if the pan is too hot, the rolls can burn. So watch the heat carefully and adjust it as needed.

CHANGE IT UP: Chocolate lovers might like to substitute miniature semisweet chocolate chips for all the pecans or use 2 tablespoons of each.

GOOD-FOR-YOU GRANOLA "PIZZAS"

PREP TIME: 20 Minutes • **START TO FINISH:** 40 Minutes • **MAKES:** 4 mini "pizzas"

2 cups oats and honey granola

¼ cup butter, melted

2 tablespoons honey

2 containers (5 oz each) vanilla French-style yogurt

1 cup mixed berries, such as blueberries, raspberries or sliced strawberries

2 tablespoons creamy peanut butter

2 tablespoons sliced almonds, toasted

1 Heat oven to 350°F. Lightly spray large cookie sheet with cooking spray.

2 Place granola in food processor; process 8 to 10 seconds or until coarsely ground. Transfer to medium bowl. Add butter and honey; stir until completely mixed. Form 4 rounds of mixture on cookie sheet, each about 4 inches in diameter and ½ inch thick, at least 2 inches apart. Bake 8 to 9 minutes or until lightly browned on edges. Cool completely on cookie sheet, 20 to 25 minutes.

3 When ready to serve, top each granola round with yogurt and berries. Spoon peanut butter into resealable food-storage plastic bag; seal bag. Cut off small corner of bag and gently squeeze peanut butter over berries. Top with almonds.

1 Mini "Pizza": Calories 500; Total Fat 26g (Saturated Fat 11g, Trans Fat 0g); Cholesterol 45mg; Sodium 210mg; Total Carbohydrate 57g (Dietary Fiber 4g); Protein 9g **Exchanges:** 2 Starch, ½ Fruit, 1½ Other Carbohydrate, ½ High-Fat Meat, 4 Fat **Carbohydrate Choices:** 4

KITCHEN SECRET: An easy way to drizzle peanut butter is to spoon it into a resealable food-storage plastic bag, seal, cut off a small corner and gently squeeze.

CHANGE IT UP: For a different flavor, try coconut French-style yogurt. Also, use any combination of your favorite fruits, such as kiwifruit, banana or apple.

RASPBERRY STREUSEL SNACK CAKE

PREP TIME: 15 Minutes • **START TO FINISH:** 1 Hour 55 Minutes • **MAKES:** 9 squares

2½ cups original all-purpose baking mix

¾ cup milk

½ cup granulated sugar

2 tablespoons butter, melted

1 teaspoon vanilla

1 egg

1 cup frozen raspberries (do not thaw)

1 tablespoon all-purpose flour

½ cup packed brown sugar

3 tablespoons cold butter

½ cup coarsely chopped pecans

1 Heat oven to 350°F. Spray 9-inch square pan with cooking spray.

2 In large bowl, beat 2 cups of the baking mix, the milk, granulated sugar, melted butter, vanilla and egg with electric mixer on low speed 30 seconds. Beat on medium speed 2 minutes, or until smooth. Pour into pan.

3 In small bowl, toss raspberries with flour. Sprinkle over batter.

4 In another small bowl, mix remaining ½ cup baking mix and the brown sugar. Cut in cold butter with fork until mixture looks like coarse crumbs. Stir in pecans. Sprinkle over raspberries.

5 Bake 35 to 40 minutes or until toothpick inserted in center comes out clean. Cool completely in pan on cooling rack, about 1 hour.

6 Cut into 3 rows by 3 rows.

1 Square: Calories 350; Total Fat 16g (Saturated Fat 6g, Trans Fat 0g); Cholesterol 0mg; Sodium 480mg; Total Carbohydrate 49g (Dietary Fiber 2g); Protein 5g **Exchanges:** 1½ Starch, 1½ Other Carbohydrate, 2½ Fat **Carbohydrate Choices:** 3

KITCHEN SECRET: Sprinkle this snack cake with a little powdered sugar for an easy way to dress it up.

ENERGY BALLS 3 WAYS

A cinch to make and store, these yummy little balls are an easy snack to pop in your mouth to keep you going on your busiest days. Stash a few in your purse or work bag, send some with the kiddos for a school snack or enjoy them as a late-night snack.

PREP TIPS

- **LAYER FLAVOR** For an added depth of flavor, you can toast the oats before adding them to these balls: Spread the oats in a 15x10-inch pan with sides. Bake at 350°F for 5 to 6 minutes or until golden brown. Or roll balls in finely chopped nuts or seeds before refrigerating them.

- **STIR 'EM UP** Natural butters (such as almond or cashew butter) often separate upon standing, so you need to stir them to recombine the layers before using.

- **DUMP 'N' STIR** Or if using the entire jar of nut butter, dump the separated butter into the bowl with the other ingredients and mix with a hand-held mixer, 2 to 3 minutes or until well mixed. Continue as directed.

- **HOW TO TOAST** You can purchase toasted sesame seed or toast your own: Cook in an 8-inch skillet over medium heat, stirring frequently, 2 to 3 minutes or until golden brown. Immediately remove from pan to prevent additional browning.

- **KEEP 'EM FRESH** Store energy balls in an airtight container in the refrigerator up to 2 weeks or in the freezer up to 2 months.

Energy Balls
3 Ways recipe
on next page

ENERGY BALLS 3 WAYS

PREP TIME: 20 Minutes • **START TO FINISH:** 50 Minutes • **MAKES:** 16 servings (2 balls each)

CHOCOLATE–PEANUT BUTTER ENERGY BALLS

- 1¼ cups old-fashioned oats
- 1 cup creamy peanut butter
- ¼ cup miniature semisweet chocolate chips
- 2 tablespoons vanilla protein powder
- 1 tablespoon chia seed
- 3 tablespoons honey

ALMOND BUTTER–CRANBERRY ENERGY BALLS

- 1¼ cups old-fashioned oats
- 1 cup almond butter
- 1 tablespoon flax seed
- 3 tablespoons honey
- ⅛ teaspoon salt
- ½ cup sweetened dried cranberries, chopped
- ¼ cup toasted almonds, chopped

SPICY CASHEW–SESAME ENERGY BALLS

- 1 jar (12 oz) cashew butter (about 1¼ cups)
- 1¼ cups old-fashioned oats
- 1 tablespoon vanilla protein powder
- 1 tablespoon toasted sesame seed
- ⅛ teaspoon salt
- ¼ teaspoon ground red pepper (cayenne)
- 3 tablespoons honey

① Line large cookie sheet with cooking parchment paper.

② Select the type of energy ball to prepare. In medium bowl, stir together all ingredients until well mixed. For extra crunch, roll balls in chopped nuts, sesame seed, etc., if you like. Shape into 32 (1-inch) balls. Place on cookie sheet.

③ Cover and refrigerate 30 minutes.

1 Serving (Chocolate–Peanut Butter Balls): Calories 170; Total Fat 10g (Saturated Fat 2.5g, Trans Fat 0g); Cholesterol 0mg; Sodium 75mg; Total Carbohydrate 13g (Dietary Fiber 2g); Protein 6g **Exchanges:** 1 Other Carbohydrate, 1 High-Fat Meat, ½ Fat **Carbohydrate Choices:** 1

KITCHEN SECRET: We love the depth of flavor these balls have when the oats are toasted before being mixed with the other ingredients. Spread them in a 15x10-inch pan with sides; bake at 350°F for 5 to 6 minutes or until golden brown.

KITCHEN SECRET: Natural butters such as almond butter and cashew butter often separate upon standing, so they require a lot of stirring to mix the oil back into the butter before using. If you are using one of the variations with these butters, you can save some time by dumping the natural butter into the bowl (without mixing it first) along with the other ingredients. Mix with a hand-held mixer on low for 2 to 3 minutes; continue as directed. You may find yourself with a few bonus energy balls when you mix them this way.

KITCHEN SECRET: You can purchase sesame seed toasted, which makes these balls come together fast, or you can toast your own: Place sesame seed in an 8-inch skillet and cook over medium heat, stirring frequently, 2 to 3 minutes or until golden brown. Immediately remove from the pan to prevent additional browning.

HOW TO STORE: Store in an airtight container in the refrigerator up to 2 weeks or in the freezer up to 2 months.

DARK CHOCOLATE ALMOND BARK CRUNCHIES

PREP TIME: 15 Minutes   •   **START TO FINISH:** 1 Hour 15 Minutes   •   **MAKES:** 12 servings (1 square each)

12 squares honey, cinnamon or chocolate vegan graham crackers

3 oz vegan dark or bittersweet chocolate, melted

3 tablespoons sliced almonds or walnuts, toasted

¼ cup dried cranberries, cherries or blueberries, finely chopped

① Line cookie sheet with waxed paper. Spread each cracker with 1 ½ teaspoons melted chocolate; place on waxed paper.

② Sprinkle with almonds and dried fruit; press lightly into chocolate.

③ Let stand 1 hour at room temperature or refrigerate 10 minutes before storing. Store covered at room temperature.

1 Serving: Calories 90; Total Fat 3.5g (Saturated Fat 1.5g, Trans Fat 0g); Cholesterol 0mg; Sodium 40mg; Total Carbohydrate 13g (Dietary Fiber 1g); Protein 1g **Exchanges:** ½ Starch, ½ Other Carbohydrate, ½ Fat **Carbohydrate Choices:** 1

KITCHEN SECRET: Alternate ideas for healthy toppings include sunflower seeds, cashews and raisins or dried pineapple, apricots or bananas finely chopped.

CHEWY OATMEAL SNACK BARS

PREP TIME: 15 Minutes • **START TO FINISH:** 2 Hours 15 Minutes • **MAKES:** 24 bars

½ cup butter
⅔ cup packed brown sugar
⅔ cup maple-flavored syrup
⅔ cup crunchy peanut butter
1 teaspoon vanilla
3 cups quick-cooking oats
1 cup wheat germ
1 cup graham cracker crumbs (16 squares, crushed)
1 cup cherry- or orange-flavored sweetened dried cranberries

1 Spray 13x9-inch pan with cooking spray.

2 In 2-quart saucepan, melt butter over medium heat. Stir in brown sugar and syrup; heat to boiling. Boil and stir 1 minute; remove from heat. Stir in peanut butter and vanilla until mixture is blended. Stir in remaining ingredients, mixing well. Press evenly in pan. Cover; refrigerate about 2 hours or until firm.

3 Cut into 6 rows by 4 rows.

1 Bar: Calories 220; Total Fat 9g (Saturated Fat 3.5g, Trans Fat 0g); Cholesterol 10mg; Sodium 85mg; Total Carbohydrate 30g (Dietary Fiber 2g); Protein 4g **Exchanges:** 1½ Starch, ½ Other Carbohydrate, 1½ Fat **Carbohydrate Choices:** 2

CHANGE IT UP: Honey or agave nectar can be used instead of maple-flavored syrup, and old-fashioned oats can be used instead of quick-cooking oats.

KITCHEN SECRET: Wrap individual bars in waxed paper to pop into your purse or backpack. When the hungries hit, it will be like a hug from home!

HOW TO STORE: Stored covered in the refrigerator up to 3 days.

NO-BAKE CHOCOLATE-PEANUT BUTTER CANDY BARS

PREP TIME: 15 Minutes • **START TO FINISH:** 45 Minutes • **MAKES:** 32 bars

24 creme-filled chocolate sandwich cookies

4 cups miniature marshmallows

¼ cup butter

1 cup semisweet chocolate chips (from 10- to 12-oz bag)

1 can (14 oz) sweetened condensed milk

1 bag (10 oz) peanut butter chips (1⅔ cups)

¼ cup creamy peanut butter

1 cup coarsely chopped honey-roasted peanuts

4 peanut butter crunchy granola bars (2 pouches from 8.9-oz box), crushed

1 teaspoon vegetable oil

KITCHEN SECRET: To easily crush granola bars, leave them in their pouches. Gently pound with a meat mallet or rolling pin to break them up. Or crumble them into a large resealable freezer plastic bag, then crush with a rolling pin.

CHANGE IT UP: You can substitute your favorite cocktail peanuts or dry-roasted peanuts for the honey-roasted peanuts.

1 Line 13x9-inch (3-quart) glass baking dish with foil, letting foil hang over two opposite sides of pan.

2 In food processor, crumble cookies. Cover and process until finely chopped.

3 In 2-quart saucepan, cook marshmallows and butter over low heat, stirring constantly, until melted. Stir in chopped cookies and ¾ cup of the chocolate chips until well mixed. Press into bottom of baking dish.

4 In medium microwavable bowl, microwave condensed milk and peanut butter chips uncovered on High 60 seconds, stirring once, until smooth. Stir in peanut butter. Stir in peanuts and granola bars. Spread over chocolate layer.

5 In small microwavable bowl, microwave remaining ¼ cup chocolate chips and the oil uncovered on High 30 seconds or until chips can be stirred smooth. Drizzle chocolate diagonally over peanut butter layer. Refrigerate until set.

6 Transfer bars from pan to cutting board, using foil to lift. Cut into 8 rows by 4 rows.

1 Bar: Calories 220; Total Fat 10g (Saturated Fat 4g, Trans Fat 0g); Cholesterol 10mg; Sodium 110mg; Total Carbohydrate 28g (Dietary Fiber 1g); Protein 3g **Exchanges:** 1 Starch, 1 Other Carbohydrate, 2 Fat **Carbohydrate Choices:** 2

NO-BAKE PUFFED QUINOA AND FRUIT BARS

PREP TIME: 20 Minutes • **START TO FINISH:** 1 Hour 10 Minutes • **MAKES:** 12 bars

½ cup dried cherries

1 tablespoon plus ½ teaspoon coconut oil

1 tablespoon agave nectar

1 tablespoon very hot water

¾ cup puffed quinoa

⅓ cup coarsely chopped roasted, salted pistachio nuts

⅓ cup plus 1 tablespoon slivered almonds

⅓ cup chopped dried apricots

½ cup vegan semisweet chocolate chips

¼ teaspoon flaked sea salt

KITCHEN SECRET: You can find puffed quinoa in many co-ops or health food stores, or online. You can also make your own: Heat a Dutch oven or 4-quart saucepan over medium-low heat 3 minutes. Add ¾ cup uncooked dry quinoa. Reduce heat to low. Stir the quinoa constantly 3 to 5 minutes until golden and puffed. Immediately transfer the puffed quinoa to rimmed baking sheet to cool.

COOKING GLUTEN FREE OR VEGAN? Always read labels to make sure *each* recipe ingredient is gluten free or vegan. Products and ingredient sources can change.

1 Line 8×4-inch loaf pan with foil, letting foil hang over two opposite sides of pan. Spray foil on bottom and sides of pan with cooking spray.

2 In bowl of small food processor, place cherries, 1 tablespoon of the coconut oil, the agave nectar and hot water. Cover; process 1 to 2 minutes or until thick paste forms.

3 In medium microwavable bowl, stir together puffed quinoa, pistachio nuts, ⅓ cup of the almonds and the apricots. Stir in cherry mixture until evenly mixed. Microwave uncovered on High 2 to 3 minutes, stirring after 1 minute, until mixture is very warm. Spread in pan using rubber spatula.

4 Freeze uncovered 30 minutes.

5 In small microwavable bowl, microwave chocolate chips and ½ teaspoon coconut oil uncovered on High 30 seconds to 1 minute, stirring after 20 seconds, until chocolate is melted and smooth. Spread evenly over bars. Finely chop remaining 1 tablespoon almonds. Sprinkle almonds and sea salt evenly over bars. Refrigerate uncovered 20 minutes or until chocolate is set.

6 Transfer bars from pan to cutting board, using foil to lift. Gently pull foil away from sides of bars. Cut into 4 rows by 3 rows.

1 Bar: Calories 170; Total Fat 7g (Saturated Fat 2.5g, Trans Fat 0g); Cholesterol 0mg; Sodium 65mg; Total Carbohydrate 22g (Dietary Fiber 2g); Protein 3g **Exchanges:** 1 Starch, ½ Other Carbohydrate, 1½ Fat **Carbohydrate Choices:** 1½

KITCHEN SECRET: These bars are vegan friendly and gluten free. If you're not worried about making them vegan, feel free to substitute honey for the agave nectar.

CINNAMON-WAFFLE CONE SNACK MIX

PREP TIME: 15 Minutes • **START TO FINISH:** 45 Minutes • **MAKES:** 24 servings (½ cup each)

6 cups cinnamon-toast flavor cereal

6 waffle-style ice cream cones, broken into small pieces

1 cup white vanilla baking chips (from 12-oz bag)

¼ cup rainbow mix candy sprinkles

1½ cups candy-coated chocolate candies

1 In large bowl, mix cereal and waffle cone pieces. Spread on waxed paper.

2 In small microwavable bowl, place baking chips. Microwave uncovered on Medium (50%) 1 minute; stir. Continue microwaving in 15-second increments, stirring after every 15 seconds, just until chips start to melt and can be stirred smooth. Transfer to small resealable food-storage plastic bag; seal bag. Cut off small corner of bag and squeeze onto cereal mixture; top with candy sprinkles. Let stand until set, about 30 minutes.

3 Break up; add chocolate candies.

1 Serving: Calories 170; Total Fat 6g (Saturated Fat 4g, Trans Fat 0g); Cholesterol 0mg; Sodium 90mg; Total Carbohydrate 26g (Dietary Fiber 1g); Protein 1g **Exchanges:** ½ Starch, 1½ Other Carbohydrate, 1 Fat **Carbohydrate Choices:** 2

KITCHEN SECRET: For best results, when breaking waffle cones, use your fingers to break each cone into smaller pieces.

CHANGE IT UP: For a sweet and salty twist, add semisweet chocolate chunks and salted peanuts to the mix. Yum!

HOW TO STORE: Easy does it! Store in an airtight container at room temperature up to 3 days, or freeze for longer storage, up to 2 weeks.

BIRTHDAY CAKE POPCORN

PREP TIME: 15 Minutes • **START TO FINISH:** 45 Minutes • **MAKES:** 13 servings (1 cup each)

8 cups popped popcorn

1 bag (12 oz) white vanilla baking chips

3 to 5 drops blue gel food color

2 tablespoons vanilla instant pudding and pie filling mix (from 3.4-oz package)

4 teaspoons rainbow-colored nonpareils

1 cup birthday cake graham snacks

1 Line two 15x10-inch pans with sides with waxed paper.

2 In large bowl, place popcorn. In medium microwavable bowl, place baking chips. Microwave chips uncovered on High 1 to 2 minutes, stirring every 30 seconds, until chips can be stirred smooth. Add food color to melted chips; mix until evenly colored. Pour chip mixture over popcorn; mix well. Sprinkle with pudding mix and nonpareils; mix well to coat.

3 Spread popcorn mixture in pans, separating popcorn pieces slightly. Let stand until set, about 30 minutes.

4 Break into bite-size clusters. Transfer to large serving bowl. Stir in graham snacks.

1 Serving: Calories 200; Total Fat 10g (Saturated Fat 6g, Trans Fat 0g); Cholesterol 0mg; Sodium 150mg; Total Carbohydrate 25g (Dietary Fiber 0g); Protein 3g **Exchanges:** 1 Starch, ½ Other Carbohydrate, 2 Fat **Carbohydrate Choices:** 1½

KITCHEN SECRET: Microwave white vanilla baking chips just until they start to melt to avoid having them seize because of overheating. Also, to have control over the look you want, start by mixing in a few dots of food color, then add more if needed.

CHANGE IT UP: Swap the blue with red gel food color to tint popcorn pink. Or divide the melted chips in half and tint some blue and some pink for a fun snack to serve at a baby shower!

HOW TO STORE: Store in airtight container at room temperature up to 3 days.

20 Minutes or Less **Sweet**

CHOCOLATE-PEANUT BUTTER SNACK MIX

PREP TIME: 20 Minutes   •   **START TO FINISH:** 20 Minutes   •   **MAKES:** 30 servings (½ cup each)

9 cups bite-size squares oven-toasted rice or corn cereal

1 cup semisweet chocolate chips (from 12-oz bag)

½ cup creamy peanut butter

¼ cup butter

1 teaspoon gluten-free vanilla

1½ cups powdered sugar

3 cups gluten-free chocolate–peanut butter O-shaped oat cereal

32 miniature gluten-free peanut butter cups, unwrapped, cut in half

1 cup salted cocktail peanuts

1 In large bowl, place rice cereal. In 1-quart microwavable bowl, microwave chocolate chips, peanut butter and butter uncovered on High 1 minute to 1 minute 30 seconds, stirring every 30 seconds, until smooth. Stir in vanilla until well mixed. Pour chocolate mixture over cereal; stir until well coated. Pour into 2-gallon resealable food-storage plastic bag; add powdered sugar. Seal bag; shake until well coated.

2 Add remaining ingredients. Seal bag; shake until well mixed.

1 Serving: Calories 200; Total Fat 10g (Saturated Fat 3.5g, Trans Fat 0g); Cholesterol 0mg; Sodium 150mg; Total Carbohydrate 23g (Dietary Fiber 1g); Protein 4g **Exchanges:** 1½ Starch, 2 Fat **Carbohydrate Choices:** 1½

CHANGE IT UP: Add gluten-free candy-coated chocolate candies or gluten-free candy-coated peanut butter pieces for added chocolate and peanut butter flavor instead of the peanut butter cups.

HOW TO STORE: Store in an airtight container in the refrigerator up to 3 days.

COOKING GLUTEN FREE? Always read labels to make sure *each* recipe ingredient is gluten free. Products and ingredient sources can change.

RAINBOW SHEBANG SNACK MIX

PREP TIME: 15 Minutes • **START TO FINISH:** 30 Minutes • **MAKES:** 16 servings (about ½ cup each)

- 4 cups bite-size squares oven-toasted rice cereal
- 1 cup fruit-flavored sweetened corn puffs cereal
- 1½ cups white vanilla baking chips (from 12-oz package)
- 1 package (2.17 oz) gluten-free, vegan candy-coated fruit-flavored chewy candies (about ⅓ cup)
- 2 tablespoons gluten-free tiny tangy rainbow crunchy candies
- 1 teaspoon rainbow-colored nonpareils

1. Line 15x10-inch pan with sides with waxed paper.

2. In large bowl, place cereals. In small microwavable bowl, microwave baking chips uncovered on High 45 seconds; stir. Microwave 30 seconds to 1 minute longer, stirring every 15 seconds, just until chips can be stirred smooth. Pour over cereal mixture; mix well until evenly coated.

3. Spread mixture in pan; sprinkle with both candies and nonpareils. Let stand until set, about 15 minutes.

4. Carefully break into bite-size pieces.

1 Serving: Calories 140; Total Fat 4.5g (Saturated Fat 3.5g, Trans Fat 0g); Cholesterol 0mg; Sodium 100mg; Total Carbohydrate 22g (Dietary Fiber 0g); Protein 1g **Exchanges:** ½ Starch, 1 Other Carbohydrate, 1 Fat **Carbohydrate Choices:** 1½

CHANGE IT UP: Substitute gluten-free fruit-flavored popping candy in place of the rainbow crunchy candies for a fun twist!

KITCHEN SECRET: Make this for your child's next birthday, movie night or slumber party. It's sure to be a hit!

HOW TO STORE: Store in a covered container at room temperature up to 5 days.

COOKING GLUTEN FREE? Always read labels to make sure *each* recipe ingredient is gluten free. Products and ingredient sources can change.

SUGARED ROSEMARY SNACK MIX

PREP TIME: 15 Minutes • **START TO FINISH:** 1 Hour 30 Minutes • **MAKES:** 12 servings (½ cup each)

1 cup organic sugar

1 tablespoon chopped fresh or 2 teaspoons dried rosemary leaves

2 teaspoons grated lemon zest

¼ teaspoon ground red pepper (cayenne)

2 cups gluten-free pretzel twists

2 cups gluten-free bite-size squares oven-toasted rice or corn cereal

1 cup whole roasted, salted cashews

1 egg white

1 teaspoon water

1 cup yogurt-covered raisins

1 Heat oven to 250°F. Generously spray 15x10-inch pan with sides with cooking spray.

2 In medium bowl, stir together sugar, rosemary, lemon zest and red pepper.

3 In large bowl, mix pretzel twists, rice cereal and cashews. In small bowl, mix egg white and water with whisk until foamy. Pour over pretzel mixture; stir with spoon or rubber spatula until evenly coated.

4 Stir sugar mixture into pretzel mixture until evenly coated. Spread pretzel mixture in single layer in pan.

5 Bake 1 hour, stirring every 15 minutes, until mixture is dry. Cool 15 minutes.

6 Stir in raisins.

1 Serving: Calories 250; Total Fat 8g (Saturated Fat 3.5g, Trans Fat 0g); Cholesterol 0mg; Sodium 190mg; Total Carbohydrate 40g (Dietary Fiber 1g); Protein 3g **Exchanges:** 2½ Other Carbohydrate, ½ High-Fat Meat, 1 Fat **Carbohydrate Choices:** 2½

COOKING GLUTEN FREE? Always read labels to make sure *each* recipe ingredient is gluten free. Products and ingredient sources can change.

KITCHEN SECRET: Save time by using the microwave. Follow directions above, except in step 3, place pretzel mixture in large microwavable bowl. In step 4, leave mixture in bowl. Microwave uncovered on High 3 to 4 minutes, stirring after 2 minutes, until ingredients are dry and crisp. Spread on waxed paper; cool 15 minutes. Stir in raisins.

CHANGE IT UP: Substitute yogurt-covered cranberries for the raisins or switch out the lemon zest for orange or lime zest.

HOW TO STORE: Store in an airtight container at room temperature up to 5 days.

30 MINUTES OR LESS

SAVORY

BUFFALO CHICKEN EMPANADAS

PREP TIME: 30 Minutes • **START TO FINISH:** 55 Minutes • **MAKES:** 21 empanadas

⅔ cup chopped deli rotisserie chicken

⅓ cup shredded mozzarella cheese (about 3 oz)

¼ cup crumbled blue cheese (1 oz)

¼ cup finely chopped yellow onion

¼ cup Buffalo wing sauce

1 can (4.5 oz) chopped green chiles, drained

1 box (14.1 oz) refrigerated pie crusts, softened as directed on box

1 egg, slightly beaten

1. Heat oven to 375°F. Line 2 cookie sheets with cooking parchment paper.

2. In medium bowl, mix all ingredients except pie crusts and egg.

3. Unroll pie crusts. Using 3½-inch round cutter, cut circles from crusts, rerolling dough to get 21 circles total.

4. Place level tablespoon of the chicken mixture on center of each circle. Fold dough in half over filling; pinch and press edges with fork to seal or roll edges to seal. Place on cookie sheets. Prick tops of empanadas with fork to allow steam to escape.

5. Brush each empanada with beaten egg. Bake 16 to 20 minutes or until golden brown. Cool 10 minutes on cooling racks.

1 Empanada: Calories 110; Total Fat 6g (Saturated Fat 2.5g, Trans Fat 0g); Cholesterol 15mg; Sodium 220mg; Total Carbohydrate 10g (Dietary Fiber 0g); Protein 3g **Exchanges:** ½ Other Carbohydrate, ½ Lean Meat, 1 Fat **Carbohydrate Choices:** ½

KITCHEN SECRET: Serve these empanadas with celery sticks and blue cheese dressing. This tradition may have been started as a way to offer the natural cooling effect of blue cheese and the crunch of celery to offset spicy, chewy Buffalo-style wings. They pair well with these spicy, flaky empanadas, too.

KITCHEN SECRET: To make ahead, prepare as directed through step 4. Cover and refrigerate up to 2 hours. Bake as directed.

KITCHEN SECRET: Have these flavor-packed mini pockets on hand at a moment's notice: Make as directed through step 4. Place on cookie sheet and freeze 1 hour, until solid. Place frozen empanadas in a 1-gallon resealable freezer plastic bag; keep frozen until ready to bake. To bake, place frozen empanadas on a cookie sheet. Brush with egg and bake 24 to 27 minutes or until golden brown.

BEEF EMPANADITAS

PREP TIME: 25 Minutes • **START TO FINISH:** 55 Minutes • **MAKES:** 20 empanaditas

2 cups original all-purpose baking mix
½ cup hot water
¼ lb ground beef (at least 80% lean)
½ cup chunky-style salsa
1 tablespoon raisins
8 pimiento-stuffed green olives, sliced
½ teaspoon ground cumin
⅛ teaspoon ground cinnamon
1 egg
1 tablespoon water

1 Heat oven to 350°F. Line cookie sheet with cooking parchment paper.

2 In medium bowl, stir baking mix and hot water until stiff dough forms. Let stand 10 minutes.

3 Meanwhile, in 8-inch skillet, cook beef over medium-high heat 5 to 7 minutes, stirring occasionally, until thoroughly cooked; drain. Stir in salsa, raisins, olives, cumin and cinnamon; set aside.

4 Place dough on surface sprinkled with baking mix; gently roll in baking mix to coat. Shape into ball; knead 10 times. Roll dough into 13-inch round. With 3-inch round cutter, cut dough into circles. Gather dough scraps together and reroll to ⅛-inch thickness. Cut to make 20 circles total.

5 Spoon 2 to 3 teaspoons of the beef mixture onto center of each dough circle. Fold dough in half over filling; press edges firmly with fork to seal. Place 1 inch apart on cookie sheet. In small bowl, stir together egg and water until well mixed; brush mixture over tops of each empanadita.

6 Bake 14 to 16 minutes or until golden brown. Let cool and serve.

1 Empanadita: Calories 70; Total Fat 3g (Saturated Fat 1g, Trans Fat 0g); Cholesterol 15mg; Sodium 200mg; Total Carbohydrate 9g (Dietary Fiber 0g); Protein 2g **Exchanges:** ½ Starch, ½ Fat **Carbohydrate Choices:** ½

CHANGE IT UP: You can substitute ground turkey or chicken for the beef.

SPINACH-FETA NAAN PIZZAS

PREP TIME: 30 Minutes • **START TO FINISH:** 45 Minutes • **MAKES:** 4 pizzas

QUICK NAAN

- 2 teaspoons cornmeal
- 2 cups original all-purpose baking mix
- 1½ teaspoons finely chopped garlic
- ¼ cup warm water
- 1 tablespoon olive or vegetable oil
- 1 container (5.3 oz) plain Greek yogurt

SAUCE

- ¾ cup Alfredo sauce (from 15-oz jar)
- ½ cup thawed frozen chopped spinach (from 9-oz box), squeezed to drain
- 1½ teaspoons finely chopped garlic

PIZZA TOPPINGS

- 1 jar (7.5 oz) marinated artichokes, drained, coarsely chopped
- ½ cup coarsely chopped fresh tomato (1 small)
- ¼ cup crumbled feta cheese (1 oz)
- ½ cup finely shredded mozzarella cheese (2 oz)

KITCHEN SECRET: The naans can be made ahead and frozen in less than 15 minutes. Prepare as directed through step 6, then let cool completely. Place in a resealable plastic freezer bag or airtight container. Thaw at room temperature while you prepare the pizza sauce and toppings. Place the naans on cookie sheets; top and bake as directed.

1. Heat oven to 450°F. Spray 2 large cookie sheets with cooking spray. Sprinkle each pan evenly with 1 teaspoon cornmeal.

2. In medium bowl, stir baking mix and garlic until blended. Stir in water, oil and yogurt; mix until soft dough forms. On surface generously sprinkled with baking mix, knead 10 to 12 times or until dough is soft and not sticky. Cover and let stand 5 minutes.

3. Meanwhile, in small bowl, stir together all Sauce ingredients; set aside.

4. Divide dough into 4 pieces. Using a rolling pin, roll each piece into 9×5-inch oval.

5. Heat 12-inch nonstick skillet over medium heat.

6. Brush 1 side of each naan with water. Carefully place 1 naan in hot skillet, water side down. Brush top of naan with water. Cover; cook about 2 minutes, turning after 1 minute, until golden on both sides. Transfer naan to cookie sheet. Repeat with remaining naans, placing 2 naans on each cookie sheet.

7. Spread about ¼ cup Sauce to within ½ inch from edge of each naan. Top naans with artichokes and tomato. Sprinkle cheeses evenly on top of each pizza.

8. Bake 6 to 8 minutes or until cheeses are melted; serve.

1 Pizza: Calories 600; Total Fat 37g (Saturated Fat 16g, Trans Fat 2g); Cholesterol 60mg; Sodium 1350mg; Total Carbohydrate 51g (Dietary Fiber 6g); Protein 16g **Exchanges:** 3 Starch, ½ Vegetable, 1 Medium-Fat Meat, 6 Fat **Carbohydrate Choices:** 3½

KITCHEN SECRET: Prevent the pizzas from getting soggy by placing the squeezed spinach between paper towels and pressing to remove any remaining moisture.

ASIAN MEATBALLS WITH TERIYAKI GLAZE

PREP TIME: 25 Minutes • **START TO FINISH:** 40 Minutes • **MAKES:** 24 meatballs

MEATBALLS

- ½ cup plain panko crispy bread crumbs
- ¼ cup whole or 2% milk
- 1 lb ground beef (at least 80% lean)
- ¼ cup chopped green onions (4 medium)
- ¼ cup finely chopped red bell pepper
- 1½ teaspoons toasted sesame oil
- ¾ teaspoon salt
- 1 clove garlic, finely chopped
- 1 egg

TERIYAKI GLAZE

- ¾ cup water
- 3 tablespoons packed brown sugar
- 2 tablespoons soy sauce
- ¼ teaspoon ground ginger
- 1 tablespoon cornstarch
- Additional sliced green onions, if desired

1 Heat oven to 400°F. Line 15x10x1-inch pan with foil; spray with cooking spray.

2 In small bowl, mix bread crumbs and milk; let stand about 5 minutes or until milk is absorbed.

3 In medium bowl, mix beef, green onions, bell pepper, sesame oil, salt, garlic, egg and bread crumb mixture. Gently stir, taking care not to compress mixture. Shape mixture into 24 (1¼-inch) balls; place on pan.

4 Bake 18 to 20 minutes or until thoroughly cooked and no longer pink in center.

5 Meanwhile, in 8-inch nonstick skillet, mix ½ cup plus 2 tablespoons of the water, the sugar, soy sauce and ginger over medium heat; heat to simmering. In small bowl, beat remaining 2 tablespoons water and the cornstarch with whisk. Add cornstarch mixture to simmering soy sauce mixture; cook 1 to 2 minutes or until thickened. Pour into medium serving bowl. Add meatballs to glaze; stir gently to coat. Sprinkle with additional sliced green onions.

1 Meatball: Calories 60; Total Fat 3g (Saturated Fat 1g, Trans Fat 0g); Cholesterol 20mg; Sodium 160mg; Total Carbohydrate 4g (Dietary Fiber 0g); Protein 4g **Exchanges:** ½ Lean Meat, ½ Fat **Carbohydrate Choices:** 0

KITCHEN SECRET: You can freeze any leftover meatballs and glaze in a microwavable food storage container up to 2 to 3 months. To reheat, microwave on High, stirring occasionally, until thoroughly heated.

MINI ASIAN SLIDERS: Prepare as directed except after shaping the beef mixture into balls in step 3, press into ½-inch-thick patties. Bake as directed until a meat thermometer inserted in the center of patties reads 165°F. Sandwich between two hot cooked potato nuggets and add desired toppings; secure with toothpicks. Serve with sweet Thai chili sauce.

TENNESSEE HOT FRIED CHICKEN TENDERS

PREP TIME: 25 Minutes • **START TO FINISH:** 25 Minutes • **MAKES:** 4 servings

1 package (14 oz) uncooked chicken tenders (not breaded)

1 teaspoon salt

½ teaspoon black pepper

1 cup all-purpose flour

½ cup buttermilk

1 teaspoon red pepper sauce

2 cups vegetable oil

3 tablespoons butter

1 teaspoon paprika

½ to 1 teaspoon ground red pepper (cayenne)

¼ teaspoon garlic powder

Sliced white sandwich bread, if desired

Sweet pickles, if desired

KITCHEN SECRET: How hot is Tennessee hot? It's up to you. We suggest a range of ground red pepper from ½ to 1 teaspoon. At the lower end of the range, you will feel it, but it won't be overwhelming. At the upper end, you will definitely get a more intense heat.

KITCHEN SECRET: To cool the heat a bit, you can serve your favorite ranch dressing alongside these tenders as a dipping sauce.

1. Sprinkle chicken tenders with ½ teaspoon of the salt and ¼ teaspoon of the black pepper.

2. In shallow bowl, mix flour, remaining ½ teaspoon salt and remaining ¼ teaspoon black pepper with whisk. In another shallow bowl, beat buttermilk and red pepper sauce together with whisk. One at a time, coat chicken tenders in seasoned flour, then in buttermilk mixture, then again in flour. Place on plate in single layer until all tenders are coated.

3. In 12-inch skillet, heat oil over medium-high heat until hot (350°F). Line 15x10x1-inch pan with paper towels; place 15x10-inch cooling rack on top of towels and cover rack with more paper towels.

4. Add all tenders to hot oil in single layer and fry about 5 minutes, turning once, until deep golden-brown outside and no longer pink in center. Using tongs, transfer to rack to drain.

5. In 1-quart saucepan, melt butter over medium-low heat. Stir in paprika, red pepper and garlic powder with whisk. Brush tops of tenders with butter mixture. Serve with slices of white bread and sweet pickles, if desired.

1 Serving: Calories 450; Total Fat 34g (Saturated Fat 10g, Trans Fat 0.5g); Cholesterol 80mg; Sodium 590mg; Total Carbohydrate 13g (Dietary Fiber 0g); Protein 23g **Exchanges:** ½ Starch, ½ Other Carbohydrate, 3 Very Lean Meat, 6½ Fat **Carbohydrate Choices:** 1

POTATO NUGGET HACKS

What is it about potato nuggets that make them so delicious and fun to eat? Can you ever have too many?

We're not sure it's possible to have too many, so we challenged ourselves to come up with some tot-tastic ways to enjoy them beyond the usual dive into the ketchup pool! Satisfy your cravings by keeping a bag of the little gems in your freezer for these irresistible ideas.

LOADED SKEWERS Thread about 5 nuggets onto each metal skewer after baking. Top nuggets with a drizzle of sour cream, crumbled cooked bacon and sliced green onions.

MINI SLIDERS Ditch the buns and use hot baked nuggets instead for mini burger bites, ham and cheese stacks or with other favorite slider fillings.

BUFFALO TOTS Toss hot baked nuggets with your favorite Buffalo wing sauce and bake a minute or two longer to heat through. Top with a drizzle of ranch dressing and blue cheese crumbles.

EGG SANDWICHES Create easy, fork-able egg sandwiches by using hot baked potato nuggets as the top and/or bottom instead of bread, a bun or an English muffin. Stuff with scrambled eggs, cooked sausage patties and cheddar cheese, or eggs Benedict ingredients (poached egg and purchased hollandaise sauce).

DIPPER DELIGHT Rather than using chips, baguette slices or other dippers for your favorite dips, why not dunk some nuggets? Try them with your favorite queso dip, salsa, guacamole or artichoke or spinach dip.

Dipper Delight

Loaded Skewers

Mini Sliders

PAN-FRIED TACO WINGS

PREP TIME: 30 Minutes • **START TO FINISH:** 30 Minutes • **MAKES:** 12 servings (2 wing pieces each)

2 eggs
2 tablespoons water
⅓ cup all-purpose flour
1 package (1 oz) original taco seasoning mix
½ teaspoon salt
¾ cup vegetable oil
2 lb chicken wings and drummettes

1 Line 15x10x1-inch pan with paper towels; place large cooling rack on top of towels.

2 In small bowl, beat eggs and water with whisk. In shallow dish, mix flour, taco seasoning mix and salt.

3 In 12-inch covered skillet, heat oil over medium-high heat until oil reaches 350°F.

4 Working in 2 batches, dip wing pieces in egg mixture to coat completely; shake off excess egg mixture, then thoroughly coat in flour mixture. Place in skillet; cover and cook 7 to 8 minutes, turning once, or until browned and juice of chicken is clear when thickest part is cut to bone (at least 165°F). Transfer to cooling rack to drain. Repeat with remaining wings and egg and flour mixtures.

1 Serving: Calories 80; Total Fat 4g (Saturated Fat 1g, Trans Fat 0g); Cholesterol 45mg; Sodium 270mg; Total Carbohydrate 4g (Dietary Fiber 0g); Protein 6g **Exchanges:** ½ Other Carbohydrate, 1 Lean Meat **Carbohydrate Choices:** 0

KITCHEN SECRET: If the wings are browning too quickly, reduce the heat to medium.

KITCHEN SECRET: Cooking wings to 175°F ensures the meat will easily come off the bone, to make them easy to eat.

KITCHEN SECRET: We suggest serving these wings with your favorite ranch dressing.

BEEFY BACON RANCH SPICY TACOS

PREP TIME: 25 Minutes • **START TO FINISH:** 35 Minutes • **MAKES:** 10 tacos

1 lb ground beef (at least 80% lean)

1 package (1 oz) original taco
seasoning mix

⅔ cup water

1 box (5.4 oz) bold spicy cheddar
taco shells

2 cups shredded lettuce

6 slices bacon, crisply cooked and
crumbled (½ cup)

½ cup diced fresh tomato

¼ cup ranch dressing

1 In 10-inch nonstick skillet, cook beef over medium heat 8 to 9 minutes, stirring occasionally, until thoroughly cooked; drain. Stir in taco seasoning mix and water. Cook 2 to 3 minutes longer or until liquid is absorbed.

2 Heat shells as directed on package. Serve with beef mixture, lettuce, bacon and tomato. Drizzle with ranch dressing.

1 Taco: Calories 210; Total Fat 13g (Saturated Fat 4.5g, Trans Fat 0g); Cholesterol 35mg; Sodium 390mg; Total Carbohydrate 11g (Dietary Fiber 0g); Protein 10g **Exchanges:** ½ Starch, 1½ Medium-Fat Meat, 1 Fat **Carbohydrate Choices:** 1

KITCHEN SECRET: Short on time? Use precooked bacon and bagged shredded lettuce to shave minutes off the prep time.

CHANGE IT UP: You can add a little extra flavor by adding 2 tablespoons thinly sliced green onions to the tacos.

CHICKEN AND AVOCADO MINI TACO BOATS

PREP TIME: 30 Minutes • **START TO FINISH:** 30 Minutes • **MAKES:** 10 taco boats

2 teaspoons vegetable oil

2 boneless skinless chicken breasts (¾ lb), cut into 1-inch pieces

⅓ cup water

2 tablespoons original taco seasoning mix (from 1-oz package)

10 mini soft flour tortilla taco boats (from 12-count package)

1 cup shredded red cabbage

⅓ cup diced avocado

¼ cup crumbled queso fresco cheese (2 oz)

2 thinly sliced green onions (2 tablespoons)

1 In 10-inch nonstick skillet, heat oil over medium heat. Add chicken; cook 5 to 7 minutes, stirring occasionally, until brown on all sides and no longer pink in center. Stir in water and taco seasoning mix; heat to boiling. Reduce heat; simmer uncovered 3 to 4 minutes, stirring frequently, until thickened.

2 Heat boats as directed on package. Divide chicken mixture among warmed boats; top with remaining ingredients.

1 Taco Boat: Calories 110; Total Fat 5g (Saturated Fat 1.5g, Trans Fat 0g); Cholesterol 25mg; Sodium 220mg; Total Carbohydrate 8g (Dietary Fiber 1g); Protein 9g **Exchanges:** ½ Starch, 1 Lean Meat, ½ Fat **Carbohydrate Choices:** ½

KITCHEN SECRET: Squeeze fresh lime juice over the filled tacos for a little extra zip.

KITCHEN SECRET: Look for bagged shredded red cabbage to cut down on prep time.

FALL HUMMUS AND VEGGIE CUTOUTS

PREP TIME: 30 Minutes   •   **START TO FINISH:** 30 Minutes   •   **MAKES:** 5 servings (¼ cup hummus, 4 pepper pieces and ½ cup veggie strips)

- 2 **large bell peppers (red, yellow or orange)**
- 1 **medium zucchini**
- 1 **large carrot**
- 1 **container (10 oz) roasted red pepper hummus**
- 2 **teaspoons chopped fresh dill weed or Italian flat-leaf parsley**

KITCHEN SECRET: A small metal canapé cutter works best for cutting shapes from bell peppers. If you don't have cutters, cut your favorite shapes with a sharp knife.

KITCHEN SECRET: Small pieces of olive can be used instead of zucchini for eyes.

KITCHEN SECRET: To make green onion curls for garnish, cut green onions into about 3-inch lengths. Cut each lengthwise into very thin strips. Place in glass of ice water to curl. Shake dry before using.

CHANGE IT UP: Instead of red pepper hummus, use your favorite flavor hummus.

COOKING GLUTEN FREE OR VEGAN? Always read labels to make sure *each* recipe ingredient is gluten free or vegan. Products and ingredient sources can change.

1 Cut tops and bottoms from bell peppers; remove seeds and membranes. Finely chop ¼ cup bell pepper from tops and bottoms; set aside. Cut into 1 pepper and spread open to form large, flat piece. With 2½- to 3-inch round metal cutter, cut circle to make base for scarecrow face. Cut remaining pepper into 1-inch-wide strips or into shapes using metal leaf cutters.

2 Cut zucchini in half lengthwise. Cut small scarecrow hat and tiny triangles for eyes from zucchini. Cut remaining zucchini into 1-inch-wide strips or into shapes using metal leaf cutters.

3 Cut carrot crosswise into 3 pieces. Cut 1 piece carrot into very thin strips or use julienne peeler to make "straw" for hair and mouth. Cut remaining pieces into 1-inch-wide strips.

4 In small serving bowl, mix hummus, reserved chopped bell pepper and dill weed; smooth top. Using photo as a guide, decorate hummus with scarecrow face. Serve with vegetable cutouts and strips.

1 Serving: Calories 140; Total Fat 5g (Saturated Fat 0.5g, Trans Fat 0g); Cholesterol 0mg; Sodium 260mg; Total Carbohydrate 17g (Dietary Fiber 5g); Protein 5g **Exchanges:** 1 Other Carbohydrate, 1 Vegetable, ½ Very Lean Meat, 1 Fat **Carbohydrate Choices:** 1

BAKED ZUCCHINI STICKS WITH PARMESAN-YOGURT DIP

PREP TIME: 25 Minutes • **START TO FINISH:** 45 Minutes • **MAKES:** 6 servings

BAKED ZUCCHINI STICKS

- 1½ cups gluten-free O-shaped toasted oat cereal
- ⅓ cup grated Parmesan cheese
- ½ teaspoon gluten-free Italian seasoning
- ⅛ teaspoon salt
  Dash pepper
- ¼ cup butter, melted
- 4 teaspoons milk
- 3 medium zucchini, cut into 3×½×½-inch sticks

PARMESAN-YOGURT DIP

- ¾ cup plain Greek yogurt
- 1 tablespoon grated Parmesan cheese
- 1 teaspoon finely chopped fresh herbs (basil, thyme or rosemary leaves)
- ¼ teaspoon salt

1 Heat oven to 400° F. Line cookie sheet with cooking parchment paper or foil.

2 Finely crush cereal. In medium bowl, stir together crushed cereal, cheese, Italian seasoning, salt and pepper. In small bowl, stir together melted butter and milk. Dip zucchini sticks in butter mixture, then roll in cereal mixture to coat evenly. Place on cookie sheet.

3 Bake about 17 minutes, turning zucchini after 9 minutes, until coating is light golden brown.

4 Meanwhile, in small bowl, stir together Parmesan-Yogurt Dip ingredients. Refrigerate until ready to serve.

1 Serving: Calories 170; Total Fat 10g (Saturated Fat 6g, Trans Fat 0g); Cholesterol 25mg; Sodium 490mg; Total Carbohydrate 12g (Dietary Fiber 2g); Protein 9g **Exchanges:** ½ Starch, ½ Vegetable, 1 Very Lean Meat, 2 Fat **Carbohydrate Choices:** 1

KITCHEN SECRET: The Parmesan-Yogurt Dip can be made up to a day ahead. Cover and refrigerate until ready to serve.

CHANGE IT UP: Make it Blue Cheese–Yogurt Dip by swapping 2 tablespoons gluten-free blue cheese crumbles for the Parmesan and adding a tablespoon or two of gluten-free blue cheese dressing to the yogurt.

KITCHEN SECRET: To easily crush cereal, place it in a resealable food-storage plastic bag or between sheets of waxed paper and crush with rolling pin or meat mallet.

COOKING GLUTEN FREE? Always read labels to make sure *each* recipe ingredient is gluten free. Products and ingredient sources can change.

GLUTEN FREE **VEGETARIAN** **PARTY READY**

ROASTED BEET HUMMUS

PREP TIME: 25 Minutes • **START TO FINISH:** 1 Hour 25 Minutes • **MAKES:** 18 servings
(2 tablespoons hummus each)

ROASTED BEETS AND GARLIC

- ½ lb uncooked red beets, peeled and cut in ½-inch wedges
- 2¼ teaspoons olive oil
- ¼ teaspoon salt
- 1 small bulb garlic

HUMMUS

- 1 can (19 oz) chick peas or garbanzo beans, drained, rinsed
- ¼ cup sesame tahini paste
- 3 tablespoons olive oil
- 2 tablespoons fresh lemon juice
- 2 tablespoons water
- ¾ teaspoon salt

TOPPINGS

- ⅓ cup crumbled feta cheese (about 3 oz)
- ¼ cup chopped toasted walnuts
- 2 tablespoons finely chopped chives
- 1 teaspoon finely grated lemon zest

1 Heat oven to 400°F. Line 15x10x1-inch pan with foil; spray with cooking spray.

2 In small bowl, toss beets with 2 teaspoons of the oil and ¼ teaspoon salt; place in single layer on pan. Remove any loose pieces of skin from garlic bulb. Place garlic on small piece of foil (about 6 inches square) and drizzle with remaining ¼ teaspoon oil. Pull sides of foil up around garlic; twist corners together to seal. Place on pan with beets.

3 Bake 35 to 40 minutes or until beets are tender and garlic is soft. Allow beets and garlic to cool 20 minutes.

4 Unwrap garlic bulb; gently squeeze 6 cloves roasted garlic into bowl of food processor. Add beets and all Hummus ingredients. Cover; process 2 to 3 minutes, scraping sides occasionally, until smooth.

5 Spoon hummus into serving bowl; top with cheese, walnuts, chives and lemon zest.

1 Serving: Calories 100; Total Fat 7g (Saturated Fat 1g, Trans Fat 0g); Cholesterol 0mg; Sodium 220mg; Total Carbohydrate 7g (Dietary Fiber 2g); Protein 3g
Exchanges: 1½ Vegetable, 1½ Fat **Carbohydrate Choices:** ½

KITCHEN SECRET: If using purchased precooked beets, reduce the beets to 6 ounces.

KITCHEN SECRET: Roasting the garlic results in a rich but milder flavor. Extra cloves of roasted garlic can be refrigerated in an airtight container up to 3 days or frozen up to 1 month.

KITCHEN SECRET: Serve hummus with gluten-free multigrain chips or fresh veggies.

COOKING GLUTEN FREE? Always read labels to make sure *each* recipe ingredient is gluten free. Products and ingredient sources can change.

GRILLSIDE GUACAMOLE

PREP TIME: 25 Minutes • **START TO FINISH:** 35 Minutes • **MAKES:** 16 servings (¼ cup each)

1 medium sweet onion, thinly sliced, cut in half

2 medium jalapeño chiles, cut in half lengthwise, seeded

4 ripe large avocados (about 2 lb) cut in half, pitted and peeled

3 plum (Roma) tomatoes, cut in half lengthwise, seeded

¼ cup chopped fresh cilantro

2 tablespoons fresh lime juice

1 clove garlic, finely chopped

1 teaspoon coarse salt (kosher or sea salt)

½ teaspoon ground cumin

¼ cup crumbled Cotija cheese (1 oz)

Tortilla chips, if desired

1 Heat gas or charcoal grill to medium heat. Spray 18x14-inch piece heavy-duty foil or grill pan with cooking spray. Place onion and chiles on foil or in pan. Place on grill over medium heat.

2 Cover grill; cook 5 to 8 minutes or until onion and jalapeños are crisp-tender and just beginning to brown. Add avocados and tomatoes to the onion and chiles. Re-cover grill; cook about 5 minutes longer, turning once halfway through, until avocados and tomatoes are hot.

3 Transfer vegetables to cutting board. Finely chop chiles and coarsely chop onions, avocados and tomatoes. In medium bowl, place all vegetables, cilantro, lime juice, garlic, salt and cumin; mix gently and thoroughly. Stir in cheese. Serve warm, with tortilla chips if desired.

1 Serving: Calories 80; Total Fat 6g (Saturated Fat 1g, Trans Fat 0g); Cholesterol 0mg; Sodium 105mg; Total Carbohydrate 5g (Dietary Fiber 3g); Protein 1g **Exchanges:** ½ Fruit, 1 Fat **Carbohydrate Choices:** ½

CHANGE IT UP: For extra heat and zing, add ¼ teaspoon red or green pepper sauce.

KITCHEN SECRET: If by some chance you find yourself with leftover guacamole (as if!), use it as a sandwich spread or a topping on your breakfast eggs.

COOKING GLUTEN FREE? Always read labels to make sure *each* recipe ingredient is gluten free. Products and ingredient sources can change

30 MINUTES OR LESS

SWEET

DECADENT VEGGIE BROWNIES

PREP TIME: 25 Minutes • **START TO FINISH:** 2 Hours 35 Minutes • **MAKES:** 16 brownies

1 medium (about 7 oz) avocado, pitted, peeled

½ cup drained diced beets (from 15-oz can)

1½ cups semisweet chocolate chips (from 12-oz bag)

3 tablespoons butter

1¼ cups whole wheat flour

¾ cup packed brown sugar

1 teaspoon baking soda

1 teaspoon vanilla

½ teaspoon salt

1 egg, beaten

1 cup semisweet chocolate chunks (from 11.5-oz bag)

1 teaspoon powdered sugar or unsweetened baking cocoa

1. Heat oven to 350°F. Spray bottom of 9-inch square pan with cooking spray.

2. In food processor, place avocado and beets. Cover and process until smooth; set aside.

3. In large microwavable bowl, microwave chocolate chips and butter uncovered on High 1 to 1½ minutes, stirring after 1 minute, until chocolate is melted. Stir in avocado mixture until well blended. Add remaining ingredients except chocolate chunks and powdered sugar; stir until well mixed. Carefully stir in chocolate chunks. Spread in pan, using rubber spatula to smooth top.

4. Bake 36 to 40 minutes or until center is set and toothpick inserted 1 inch from edge of pan comes out clean. Cool completely in pan on cooling rack, about 1½ hours.

5. Sprinkle with powdered sugar. Cut into 4 rows by 4 rows.

1 Brownie: Calories 260; Total Fat 12g (Saturated Fat 7g, Trans Fat 0g); Cholesterol 15mg; Sodium 190mg; Total Carbohydrate 36g (Dietary Fiber 3g); Protein 3g **Exchanges:** ½ Starch, 2 Other Carbohydrate, 2½ Fat **Carbohydrate Choices:** 2½

CHANGE IT UP: If you don't have chocolate chunks in your pantry, substitute more semisweet chips or milk chocolate chips. Like nuts? Add ½ cup of your favorite nut to the batter. We suggest chopped pecans or walnuts.

HOW TO STORE: Store tightly covered at room temperature up to 3 days.

JACK-O'-LANTERN BROWNIES

PREP TIME: 30 Minutes • **START TO FINISH:** 2 Hours 50 Minutes • **MAKES:** 16 brownies

1 box (16 oz) brownie mix
⅓ cup vegetable oil
3 tablespoons water
1 egg
1¼ cups creamy vanilla frosting (from 16-oz container)
　Black and orange gel food colors
8 green gumdrops, cut in half

KITCHEN SECRET: To easily line the bottom of a pan, tip it upside down and form the foil around the outside bottom and sides. Remove the foil, flip the pan over and place the foil inside the pan for a perfect fit!

KITCHEN SECRET: To cut brownies easily, use a plastic knife. Refrigerating before cutting helps ensure cleaner cuts.

KITCHEN SECRET: For pumpkins with a more Halloween feel, decorate the brownies with candies to make eyes, nose and mouth (use the photo as guide). Use assorted candies such as gumdrops, mini candy-coated chocolate candies or even candy corn!

1 Heat oven to 350°F. Line 9-inch square pan with foil, letting foil hang 2 inches over sides of pan. Grease bottom and sides of foil with shortening or cooking spray.

2 Make brownie batter as directed on box using oil, water and egg. Spread in pan.

3 Bake 28 to 31 minutes or until toothpick inserted 2 inches from side of pan comes out almost clean. Cool completely on cooling rack, about 1 hour 30 minutes.

4 Freeze in pan 30 minutes. Using foil to lift, transfer brownies to cutting board; peel away foil.

5 In small bowl, place 2 tablespoons of the frosting; tint with black food color to desired color. Place in small resealable food-storage plastic bag; partially seal bag and set aside. In another small bowl, place remaining frosting; tint with orange food color to desired color. Frost top of brownies with orange-tinted frosting. For easier cutting, refrigerate 15 minutes to set frosting.

6 Use sharp knife to cut brownies into squares, 4 rows by 4 rows, to make 16 brownies; clean knife with paper towel after each cut. Slightly separate brownies. Press gumdrop half on top edge of each brownie for stem.

7 Cut off tiny corner of black frosting bag. Squeeze bag to pipe faces.

1 Brownie: Calories 260; Total Fat 10g (Saturated Fat 2.5g, Trans Fat 0g); Cholesterol 10mg; Sodium 150mg; Total Carbohydrate 43g (Dietary Fiber 0g); Protein 1g **Exchanges:** 3 Other Carbohydrate, 2 Fat **Carbohydrate Choices:** 3

EASY CRACKER TOFFEE

PREP TIME: 30 Minutes • **START TO FINISH:** 2 Hours 50 Minutes • **MAKES:** 32 pieces

40 buttery crackers
1 cup butter
1 cup sugar
½ teaspoon salt
1 teaspoon vanilla
1 bag (11.5 oz) milk chocolate chips (2 cups)
1 tablespoon candy sprinkles

1 Heat oven to 350°F. Line 15x10x1-inch pan with foil. Spray foil with cooking spray. Place crackers in single layer on pan.

2 In 2-quart saucepan, using heat-resistant spatula, stir butter, sugar and salt over medium heat until butter is melted. Heat to boiling, stirring frequently. Boil 7 to 9 minutes longer, stirring frequently, until light brown. Remove from heat. Add vanilla; stir until blended. Immediately pour mixture evenly over crackers in pan; spread with spatula to cover.

3 Bake 13 to 15 minutes or until bubbly and brown.

4 Sprinkle chocolate chips evenly on top. Let stand 5 minutes.

5 Spread chocolate evenly over cracker mixture. Sprinkle with candy sprinkles. Cool completely, about 2 hours or until chocolate is set.

6 Break into pieces.

1 Serving: Calories 160; Total Fat 10g (Saturated Fat 6g, Trans Fat 0g); Cholesterol 20mg; Sodium 115mg; Total Carbohydrate 15g (Dietary Fiber 0g); Protein 1g **Exchanges:** 1 Other Carbohydrate, 2 Fat **Carbohydrate Choices:** 1

CHANGE IT UP: Try semisweet or dark chocolate chips for a new flavor twist!

KITCHEN SECRET: For success when making toffee, pay attention to the cooking time and toffee color for the perfect result.

HOW TO STORE: Store in a covered container in the refrigerator up to 1 week.

30 Minutes or Less **Sweet**

NO-BAKE LAYERED CINNAMON CEREAL BARS

PREP TIME: 30 Minutes • **START TO FINISH:** 1 Hour 30 Minutes • **MAKES:** 24 bars

5 cups cinnamon-toast flavor cereal

2 cups miniature marshmallows

¼ cup butter, melted

1½ cups powdered sugar

1 jar (7 oz) marshmallow creme

28 caramels (from 11-oz bag), unwrapped

¼ cup heavy whipping cream

¾ cup salted mixed nuts

¼ cup semisweet chocolate chips

¼ teaspoon vegetable oil

CHANGE IT UP: There are many blends of salted nuts available. Any blend of your favorite mixed nuts will work for this bar.

HOW TO STORE: These bars have a creamy, soft filling and should be refrigerated. Store covered in the refrigerator up to 2 days.

1 Spray 9-inch square pan with cooking spray.

2 Remove ¼ cup of the cereal; coarsely crush it and set aside.

3 In large microwavable bowl, microwave marshmallows and butter uncovered on High 1 to 2 minutes, stirring every minute, until melted and smooth. Stir in remaining 4¾ cups cereal until well coated. Press into bottom of pan.

4 In medium bowl, stir together powdered sugar and marshmallow creme until well mixed (mixture will be thick and sticky). With wet offset metal spatula, spread marshmallow creme mixture evenly over cereal mixture.

5 In small microwavable bowl, microwave caramels and cream uncovered on High 2 to 3 minutes, stirring after every minute, until melted and smooth. Cool 5 minutes.

6 Pour and evenly spread caramel over marshmallow mixture. Sprinkle with nuts and reserved crushed cereal, pressing slightly.

7 In small microwavable bowl, microwave chocolate chips and oil uncovered on High 15 to 30 seconds, stirring after 15 seconds, until melted. Drizzle chocolate over nuts. Cover and refrigerate 1 hour before cutting.

8 Cut into 6 rows by 4 rows.

1 Bar: Calories 240; Total Fat 10g (Saturated Fat 3g, Trans Fat 0g); Cholesterol 10mg; Sodium 120mg; Total Carbohydrate 35g (Dietary Fiber 1g); Protein 2g **Exchanges:** ½ Starch, 2 Other Carbohydrate, 2 Fat **Carbohydrate Choices:** 2

LADYBUG SUMMERTIME FUN SNACKS

PREP TIME: 30 Minutes　•　**START TO FINISH:** 30 Minutes　•　**MAKES:** 4 ladybugs

2　boxes (5 oz each) multicolored
　　fruit-flavored snacks

4　vanilla wafer cookies
　　Round candy sprinkles

½　cup creamy vanilla frosting
　　(from 16-oz container)

1　tube (0.68 oz) black decorating gel

1 Unroll and remove paper from desired color fruit-flavored snacks. Using 2½-inch round cutter, cut 4 circles from snacks. (A bottle or jar cap this size can also be used as a guide to cut around with knife or kitchen scissors.) Wrap cut circles around cookies.

2 To make legs, cut rectangle from portion of blue fruit-flavored snack, 3 inches long and ½-inch wide; roll up tightly. Cut into 6 (½-inch-wide) pieces. To attach legs, cut a 1½-inch circle from fruit-flavored snack. Place leg pieces on circle, attaching with small amount of frosting. Attach to bottom of covered cookie, using small amount of frosting. Place candy sprinkles on back of ladybug.

3 Attach fruit-flavored snack to top of covered cookie for head, using small amount of frosting. Place frosting in small resealable food-storage plastic bag; seal bag. Cut off tiny corner and pipe eyes on ladybug; add dot of black gel for pupil of eye. Repeat to make 3 additional ladybugs.

1 Ladybug: Calories 210; Total Fat 7g (Saturated Fat 1.5g, Trans Fat 2g); Cholesterol 0mg; Sodium 125mg; Total Carbohydrate 37g (Dietary Fiber 0g); Protein 0g **Exchanges:** 2½ Other Carbohydrate, 1½ Fat **Carbohydrate Choices:** 2½

KITCHEN SECRET: Top cupcakes with ladybugs just before serving for a birthday or summertime celebration.

KITCHEN SECRET: Ladybugs make a great edible centerpiece; place on plastic wrap or cooking parchment paper to prevent them from sticking to the plate.

FROZEN BANANA POPS

These smile makers are a satisfying indulgence for both kids and adults, alike!

Whip up a batch of banana pops, chunks or slices to keep in your freezer for an instant snack, whenever you're hungry. Use what you have on hand to create a new flavor every time.

BANANA POP TIPS

- **SKEWER** banana halves, chunks or slices with wooden craft sticks or skewers.

- **FREEZE** bananas until firm, 30 minutes to 1 hour.

- **DIP** banana pieces in nut butter, melted chocolate or Greek yogurt. Or spread with frosting if rolling or attaching other ingredients.

- **CONTAINER SAVVY** When dipping banana halves or chunks, use a tall, narrow container for the coating to dip larger pieces easily. A liquid measuring cup or mason jar works well.

- **ROLL** coated banana pieces in desired ingredients, such as crushed freeze-dried strawberries or ready-to-eat cereal, coconut, chopped nuts, sprinkles or crushed pretzels.

- **PLACE** bananas in single layer on a waxed paper–lined cookie sheet.

- **FREEZE** until coating is firm (10 to 30 minutes).

- **DRIZZLE** with nut butter, chocolate or caramel topping or melted candy melts or coating wafers, if desired; sprinkle with sprinkles, if desired. Or drizzle uncoated banana pieces but serve within 4 hours.

- **STORE 'EM** Transfer to freezer-safe food storage container and store in freezer up to 1 week.

monsters

peanut butter–peanut

melted chocolate and peanut butter

gnomes

266

tutti fruity

chocolate banana chunks

EVERYING

EVERYTHING

DIP: almond or cashew butter

ROLL: everything bagel seasoning

TUTTI FRUITY

SPREAD: chocolate frosting

ROLL: fruit-flavored sweetened corn puffs cereal

BREAKFAST BLUEBERRY

DIP: Greek yogurt

ROLL: granola and dried blueberries

MONSTERS

SPREAD: frosting (tinted, if desired)

ATTACH: googly-eye candies and coconut (tinted, if desired)

BANANA SPLITS

DIP OR SPREAD: frosting

ROLL: sprinkles

TOP: whipped cream and maraschino cherry

GNOMES

SPREAD: frosting

ATTACH: small candy for nose, coconut for beard, piece of chewy fruit snack formed into a hat and mini marshmallow tassel

MASKED TURTLES MARSHMALLOW POPS

PREP TIME: 30 Minutes • **START TO FINISH:** 30 Minutes • **MAKES:** 8 pops

1 container (16 oz) creamy vanilla frosting
Green food coloring
8 paper lollipop sticks
8 large marshmallows
4 rolls chewy fruit-flavored snack (from 4.5-oz box), any variety
16 candy eyes
1 teaspoon (from 0.68 oz tube) black decorating gel or creamy chocolate frosting (from a 6-oz container)

1 In small deep microwavable bowl, place vanilla frosting. Microwave uncovered on High 15 to 20 seconds or until frosting can be stirred smooth. Stir in food color until light green.

2 Insert 1 lollipop stick into each marshmallow; dip into frosting to evenly coat. Place in tall glass to dry, about 10 minutes.

3 Unroll fruit snack and cut about 8x½-inch strips of desired colors to make masks. Place cut strip on cutting board. Starting at midpoint of strip, use small sharp knife to cut 2 small horizontal slits for eyes, about ¾ inch apart. Place candy eyes under slits in fruit snacks. Place masks on dried marshmallows, tying to secure. Cut off ends of fruit snack strips, leaving about 1 inch remaining.

4 Use gel to draw mouths on marshmallows under masks. Or place chocolate frosting in small resealable food-storage plastic bag, seal bag, and cut off tiny corner of bag; pipe mouths on marshmallows.

1 Pop: Calories 280; Total Fat 9g (Saturated Fat 4g, Trans Fat 0g); Cholesterol 0mg; Sodium 150mg; Total Carbohydrate 51g (Dietary Fiber 0g); Protein 0g **Exchanges:** 3½ Other Carbohydrate, 2 Fat **Carbohydrate Choices:** 3½

KITCHEN SECRET: You can dry and display your pops by inserting them into a block of white plastic craft foam, which can be purchased at craft stores.

KITCHEN SECRET: Try refrigerating dipped marshmallows for 20 to 30 minutes to firm up the marshmallow before decorating.

SLOW-COOKER CARAMEL CORN

PREP TIME: 25 Minutes ● **START TO FINISH:** 2 Hours 40 Minutes ● **MAKES:** 14 servings (about 1 cup each)

½ cup butter, cut into tablespoons
1 cup packed light brown sugar
¼ cup light corn syrup
1 teaspoon baking soda
1 teaspoon vanilla
12 cups popped popcorn
2 cups mini pretzel twists
1 cup mixed nuts

1 Spray 6-quart slow cooker with cooking spray.

2 In bottom of slow cooker, layer butter, brown sugar and corn syrup. Cover and cook on High heat setting 30 minutes. Carefully remove slow cooker's insert, leaving cover on, and rotate 180 degrees; replace in cooker. Continue to cook on High heat setting another 30 minutes or until caramel mixture is bubbling vigorously around edges.

3 Remove cover; turn heat setting to Low. Stir in baking soda and vanilla with heat-resistant spatula until well blended; mixture will foam while being stirred. Add popcorn and stir well to coat, making sure to reach bottom and all around inside of slow cooker. Continue to cook, uncovered, on Low heat setting 1 hour to 1 hour 30 minutes, stirring every 15 to 20 minutes, until popcorn looks dry and caramel is cooked on.

4 Spread on waxed paper; cool 15 minutes. Stir in pretzel twists and nuts.

1 Serving: Calories 250; Total Fat 16g (Saturated Fat 5g, Trans Fat 0g); Cholesterol 15mg; Sodium 280mg; Total Carbohydrate 25g (Dietary Fiber 1g); Protein 2g **Exchanges:** ½ Starch, 1 Other Carbohydrate, 3 Fat **Carbohydrate Choices:** 1½

KITCHEN SECRET: Slow cookers vary in how they heat, so keep an eye on your caramel as it nears the end of cooking time.

CHANGE IT UP: Try your favorite combination of mix-ins to make the caramel corn your own with different nuts, candy-coated chocolate candies, dried fruit or potato chips.

HOW TO STORE: Store in an airtight container at room temperature up to 2 days.

HOT CHOCOLATE WINTER MIX

PREP TIME: 25 Minutes • **START TO FINISH:** 55 Minutes • **MAKES:** 13 servings (½ cup each)

2 cups bite-size squares oven-toasted rice or corn cereal

2 cups bite-size squares chocolate oven-toasted rice cereal

½ cup powdered sugar

3 tablespoons instant cocoa mix

1 cup semisweet chocolate chips (from 12-oz bag)

½ cup white vanilla baking chips (from 12-oz bag)

1 cup miniature marshmallows

½ cup semisweet chocolate nonpareils

KITCHEN SECRET: Chocolate nonpareils are chocolate disks covered in tiny white or colored candies; they come in small and large sizes. We used the large size in this mix; they are about 1 inch in diameter and can be purchased in the bulk candy section of the grocery store. The small size can be found in the boxed movie theater candy section.

KITCHEN SECRET: If the melted white vanilla baking chips are too hot, you may need to cool them slightly before adding marshmallows so they don't melt the marshmallows.

HOW TO STORE: Store in a covered container at room temperature up to 2 days.

1 Line two 15x10x1-inch pans with sides with waxed paper.

2 In large bowl, mix cereals. In small bowl, mix powdered sugar and cocoa mix.

3 In small microwavable bowl, microwave chocolate chips uncovered on High 45 seconds; stir. Continue microwaving in 15-second increments, stirring after every 15 seconds, until chips are melted and smooth. Pour onto cereal in bowl; mix thoroughly to coat. Transfer mixture to 2-gallon resealable food-storage plastic bag; add powdered sugar mixture to bag. Seal bag; shake to coat thoroughly. Spread in one of the pans to cool completely, about 30 minutes.

4 While cereal is cooling, in small microwavable bowl, microwave baking chips uncovered on High 30 seconds; stir. Continue microwaving in 15-second increments, stirring after every 15 seconds, just until chips start to melt and can be stirred smooth. Stir in marshmallows to coat completely. Spread in second pan, leaving marshmallows into small clusters. Let stand until set, about 30 minutes.

5 In large serving bowl, mix cereal, marshmallow clusters and chocolate nonpareils.

1 Serving: Calories 200; Total Fat 7g (Saturated Fat 4.5g, Trans Fat 0g); Cholesterol 0mg; Sodium 105mg; Total Carbohydrate 33g (Dietary Fiber 1g); Protein 2g **Exchanges:** ½ Starch, 1½ Other Carbohydrate, 1½ Fat **Carbohydrate Choices:** 2

CHANGE IT UP: Add a peppermint twist to your mix by stirring in ¼ cup crushed peppermint candy. If you want more chocolate flavor, add ¼ cup chocolate chunks to the mix.

COCONUT-CHOCOLATE-COVERED CHEESECAKE BITES

PREP TIME: 25 Minutes • **START TO FINISH:** 3 Hours • **MAKES:** 32 bites

4 tablespoons shortening

10 to 12 creme-filled chocolate sandwich cookies (from an 11-oz package), crushed (1 cup)

1 package (8 oz) cream cheese, softened

⅓ cup sugar

1 egg

1 teaspoon coconut extract

1 cup semisweet chocolate chips (from 12-oz bag)

2 tablespoons shredded coconut, toasted if desired

1 Bite: Calories 100; Total Fat 6g (Saturated Fat 3g, Trans Fat 0g); Cholesterol 15mg; Sodium 40mg; Total Carbohydrate 8g (Dietary Fiber 0g); Protein 1g **Exchanges:** ½ Starch, 1 Fat **Carbohydrate Choices:** ½

KITCHEN SECRET: A 2-cup glass measuring cup works great for melting the chocolate mixture and dipping the cheesecake bites. When using tongs to dip, wipe the ends with a paper towel every so often to remove the excess chocolate mixture that builds up while dipping.

KITCHEN SECRET: To toast coconut, heat oven to 350°F. Spread coconut in ungreased shallow pan. Bake 5 to 7 minutes, stirring occasionally, until golden brown. Cool.

1 Heat oven to 325°F. Line 9x5-inch loaf pan with foil, letting foil hang over two long sides of pan by about 1 inch.

2 In small microwavable bowl, microwave 2 tablespoons of the shortening on High 15 seconds or until melted. Stir in cookie crumbs. Pat crumb mixture evenly onto bottom of pan.

3 In medium bowl, beat cream cheese with electric mixer on medium speed until fluffy. Beat in sugar until well blended. Beat in egg and coconut extract on low speed until smooth. Spread cream cheese mixture evenly over crumb mixture. Bake 25 minutes or just until set. Cool on cooling rack 30 minutes.

4 Cover and freeze cheesecake 1 hour or until cold and firm enough to cut.

5 Line cookie sheet with waxed paper. Transfer cheesecake from pan to cutting board by lifting foil; peel away foil. With sharp knife, cut into 8 rows by 4 rows. Separate pieces and place on cookie sheet. Place uncovered in freezer while making chocolate coating.

6 In small microwavable bowl, microwave chocolate chips and remaining 2 tablespoons shortening on High 1 minute to 1 minute 30 seconds, stirring after 1 minute, until chocolate is melted and smooth.

7 Using tongs or fork, dip top and sides of a cheesecake square in chocolate mixture to coat. Return to cookie sheet crust down. Sprinkle immediately with coconut. Repeat with remaining cheesecake squares, chocolate and coconut. Refrigerate at least 30 minutes or until chocolate is set.

RASPBERRY CREAM-FILLED CHOCOLATES

PREP TIME: 30 Minutes • **START TO FINISH:** 55 Minutes • **MAKES:** 12 chocolates

1¼ cups dark chocolate chips (from 10-oz bag)
1 teaspoon vegetable oil
2 oz gluten-free cream cheese (from 8-oz package), softened
1 tablespoon sugar
¼ teaspoon vanilla
12 fresh raspberries (about ½ cup)

KITCHEN SECRET: Small raspberries work best for these so the chocolate can cover them completely.

CHANGE IT UP: Semisweet or milk chocolate chips may be substituted for the dark chocolate chips in this recipe.

HOW TO STORE: Store in a covered container in the refrigerator up to 5 days, as the filling needs to be kept cool.

COOKING GLUTEN FREE? Always read labels to make sure *each* recipe ingredient is gluten free. Products and ingredient sources can change.

1. Place a mini paper baking cup or paper candy cup in each of 12 mini muffin cups.

2. In medium microwavable bowl, microwave chocolate chips and oil uncovered on High 1 minute to 1 minute 30 seconds, stirring every 30 seconds, until smooth. Spoon 1 teaspoon of the chocolate into bottom of each muffin cup. Refrigerate 15 minutes or until chocolate is set.

3. Meanwhile, in small bowl, beat cream cheese, sugar and vanilla with electric mixer on medium speed until smooth and creamy.

4. Spoon 1 teaspoon of the cream cheese mixture evenly in center of each chocolate-lined muffin cup. Place 1 raspberry in center of cream cheese mixture, pressing in slightly. Spoon remaining chocolate evenly over raspberries, about 2 teaspoons per cup, covering berries completely. Refrigerate 20 minutes or until set.

5. Let stand at room temperature 3 minutes before serving.

1 Chocolate: Calories 120; Total Fat 7g (Saturated Fat 4.5g, Trans Fat 0g); Cholesterol 5mg; Sodium 20mg; Total Carbohydrate 12g (Dietary Fiber 1g); Protein 1g **Exchanges:** ½ Starch, ½ Other Carbohydrate, 1½ Fat **Carbohydrate Choices:** 1

METRIC CONVERSION GUIDE

VOLUME

U.S. UNITS		CANADIAN METRIC		AUSTRALIAN METRIC	
¼	teaspoon	1	mL	1	ml
½	teaspoon	2	mL	2	ml
1	teaspoon	5	mL	5	ml
1	tablespoon	15	mL	20	ml
¼	cup	50	mL	60	ml
⅓	cup	75	mL	80	ml
½	cup	125	mL	125	ml
⅔	cup	150	mL	170	ml
¾	cup	175	mL	190	ml
1	cup	250	mL	250	ml
1	quart	1	liter	1	liter
1½	quarts	1.5	liters	1.5	liters
2	quarts	2	liters	2	liters
2½	quarts	2.5	liters	2.5	liters
3	quarts	3	liters	3	liters
4	quarts	4	liters	4	liters

WEIGHT

U.S. UNITS	CANADIAN METRIC		AUSTRALIAN METRIC	
1 ounce	30	grams	30	grams
2 ounces	55	grams	60	grams
3 ounces	85	grams	90	grams
4 ounces (¼ pound)	115	grams	125	grams
8 ounces (½ pound)	225	grams	225	grams
16 ounces (1 pound)	455	grams	500	grams
1 pound	455	grams	0.5	kilogram

MEASUREMENTS

INCHES	CENTIMETERS
1	2.5
2	5.0
3	7.5
4	10.0
5	12.5
6	15.0
7	17.5
8	20.5
9	23.0
10	25.5
11	28.0
12	30.5
13	33.0

TEMPERATURES

FAHRENHEIT	CELSIUS
32°	0°
212°	100°
250°	120°
275°	140°
300°	150°
325°	160°
350°	180°
375°	190°
400°	200°
425°	220°
450°	230°
475°	240°
500°	260°

NOTE: The recipes in this cookbook have not been developed or tested using metric measures. When converting recipes to metric, some variations in quality may be noted.

INDEX

Note: Page references in *italics* indicate photographs.

A

Almond butter
Energy Balls 3 Ways, *205*, 206

Almond(s)
Banana-Coconut Yogurt Cup, *56*, 57
Bark Crunchies, Dark Chocolate, 207
Caramelized Banana Bowl, *84*, 85
Raspberry Chocolate Hazelnut Cereal "Nachos," 76
Spicy Caramel Corn Snack Mix, 98, *99*

Apple(s)
Fruit Fish, *64*, 65
Spiced Pumpkin, and Jalapeño Dip, 194, *195*

Artichoke(s)
and Jalapeño Cheese Spread, Baked, 48, *49*
and Spinach Dip, Spicy, *168*, 169
Spinach-Feta Naan Pizzas, *230*, 231

Avocado(s)
Beer Queso Nachos, *132*, 133
and Chicken Mini Taco Boats, 242, *243*
Decadent Veggie Brownies, 256, *257*
Grilled Bean Chip Nachos, *130*, 131
Grillside Guacamole, 250, *251*
"Jalapeño Popper" Boats, *108*, 109
-Salsa Cheese Snacks, *16*, 17

B

Bacon
Cheeseburger Dip, Slow-Cooker, *178*, 179
-Chipotle Dip, Blooming Onion with, 156, *157*
Jalapeño Turkey Roll-Ups, *110*, 111

Loaded Baked Potato Nachos, 128, *129*
Mac and Cheese Bowl, 22, *23*
Ranch Spicy Tacos, Beefy, *240*, 241

Banana(s)
Caramelized, Bowl, *84*, 85
-Coconut Yogurt Cup, *56*, 57
Honey Chai-Spiced Pan-Fried, *92*, 93
-Mango and Oat "Milk" Smoothies, *73*, 75
–Peanut Butter Bites with Mini Marshmallows, 90, *91*
Pops, Frozen, 266–67, *266–67*
Split Yogurt Cups, Turtle, 58, *59*

Bars
Candy, No-Bake Chocolate–Peanut Butter, *210*, 211
Cereal, No-Bake Layered Cinnamon, 262, *263*
Chewy Oatmeal Snack, 208, *209*
Decadent Veggie Brownies, 256, *257*
Jack-O'-Lantern Brownies, *258*, 259
Puffed Quinoa and Fruit, No-Bake, 212, *213*

Basil
-Cheese Triangles, *124*, 125
Savory Caprese Bowl, *18*, 19
-Spinach Dip, 166, *167*
and Sun-Dried Tomato Yogurt Bark, 160, 161

Bean Chip Nachos, Grilled, *130*, 131

Bean(s)
Beer Queso Nachos, *132*, 133
Chick Pea and Veggie Burgers, *116*, 117
Easy Hummus, *33*, 34
Fire-Roasted Tomato Hummus, *38*, 39
French Bread Taco Pizza, *138*, 139
Greek-Style Cottage Cheese Snack Bowl, 20, *21*
Green, "Fries," Spicy, 28, *29*
Roasted, 3 Ways, *147*, 148
Roasted Beet Hummus, *248*, 249
roasting, tips for, 146
Tex-Mex Tailgate Dip, 180, *181*

RECIPE TESTING AND CALCULATING NUTRITION INFORMATION

RECIPE TESTING:

- Large eggs and 2% milk were used unless otherwise indicated.

- Fat-free, low-fat, low-sodium or "lite" products were not used unless indicated.

- No nonstick cookware and bakeware were used unless indicated. No dark-colored, black or insulated bakeware was used.

- When a pan is specified, a metal pan was used; a baking dish or pie plate means ovenproof glass was used.

- An electric hand mixer was used for mixing only when mixer speeds are specified.

CALCULATING NUTRITION:

- The first ingredient was used wherever a choice is given, such as ⅓ cup sour cream or plain yogurt.

- The first amount was used whenever a range is given, such as a 3- to 3½-pound whole chicken.

- The first serving number was used whenever a range is given, such as 4 to 6 servings.

- "If desired" ingredients were not included.

- Only the amount of a marinade or frying oil that is absorbed was included.

- Diabetic exchanges are not calculated in recipes containing uncooked alcohol, due to its effect on blood sugar levels.

Bean(s) (cont.)

White, Hummus–Filled Vegetables with Gremolata, 174, *175*

Beef

Asian Meatballs with Teriyaki Glaze, 232, *233*

Beefy Bacon Ranch Spicy Tacos, *240,* 241

Empanaditas, *228,* 229

French Bread Taco Pizza, *138,* 139

and Green Chile, Cheesy, Spicy Tacos, *114,* 115

Slow-Cooker Bacon Cheeseburger Dip, *178,* 179

Beer

Cheese Dip, *170,* 171

Queso Nachos, *132,* 133

Beet(s)

Decadent Veggie Brownies, 256, *257*

Roasted, Hummus, *248,* 249

Berries. *See also* **Cranberries; Raspberry; Strawberry(ies)**

Blueberry Crunch Parfait, *86,* 87

Galactic Fro-Yo Bark, 186, *187*

Good-for-You Granola "Pizzas," 200, *201*

Birthday Cake Popcorn, *216,* 217

Blueberry(ies)

Crunch Parfait, *86,* 87

Galactic Fro-Yo Bark, 186, *187*

Bourbon-Honey BBQ Wings, Slow-Cooker, *142,* 143

Bread

Feta and Spinach–Stuffed, 136, *137*

French, Taco Pizza, *138,* 139

Brownie Cups, Salted Caramel Macchiato, 96, *97*

Brownies

Decadent Veggie, 256, *257*

Jack-O'-Lantern, *258,* 259

"Bruschetta," Tzatziki, *152,* 153

Buffalo Chicken Dip, 42, *43*

Buffalo Chicken Empanadas, 226, *227*

Buffalo Veggie–Stuffed Mushrooms, 154, *155*

Burgers, Chick Pea and Veggie, *116,* 117

Cake Mix, Easy Scratch, 77

Cakes

Mug, Confetti, *78, 79*

Mug, Cookie Butter, 80, *81*

Snack, Raspberry Streusel, 202, *203*

Caprese Bowl, Savory, *18,* 19

Caramel Corn Snack Mix, Spicy, 98, *99*

Caramelized Banana Bowl, *84,* 85

Carrot(s)

Fall Hummus and Veggie Cutouts, 244, *245*

"Fries," Italian, 30, *31*

Cashews or cashew butter

Energy Balls 3 Ways, *205,* 206

Sugared Rosemary Snack Mix, 222, *223*

Cauliflower

Buffalo Veggie–Stuffed Mushrooms, 154, *155*

Cheddar "Popcorn," *26,* 27

Celebration Snack Mix, *102,* 103

Cereal-based snacks

Baked Zucchini Sticks with Parmesan-Yogurt Dip, *246,* 247

Blooming Onion with Bacon-Chipotle Dip, 156, *157*

Blueberry Crunch Parfait, *86,* 87

Celebration Snack Mix, *102,* 103

Chocolate–Peanut Butter Snack Mix, *218,* 219

Cinnamon–Waffle Cone Snack Mix, *214,* 215

Citrus Crunch Parfait, 68, *69*

Coconut-Berry "Bubble" Parfait, *52, 53*

Galactic Fro-Yo Bark, 186, *187*

Hot Chocolate Winter Mix, 272, *273*

Loaded Baked Potato Nachos, 128, *129*

No-Bake Layered Cinnamon Cereal Bars, 262, *263*

Peanut Butter–Banana Bites with Mini Marshmallows, 90, *91*

Quick Peach "Cobbler" Snack, *94,* 95

Rainbow Shebang Snack Mix, 220, *221*

Raspberry Chocolate Hazelnut Cereal "Nachos," 76

Strawberry-Lemon Shortcake Bowl, 66, *67*

Sugared Rosemary Snack Mix, 222, *223*

Ultimate Tailgate Party Mix, 46, 47

White Chocolate-Drizzled Cereal Mix, *100,* 101

Chai Latte, Iced Oat "Milk," *72,* 74

Chai-Spiced Honey Pan-Fried Bananas, *92,* 93

Cheese

Avocado "Jalapeño Popper" Boats, *108,* 109

Bacon Jalapeño Turkey Roll-Ups, *110,* 111

Bacon Mac and, Bowl, 22, *23*

Baked Zucchini Sticks with Parmesan-Yogurt Dip, *246,* 247

-Basil Triangles, *124,* 125

Beer Dip, *170,* 171

Beer Queso Nachos, *132,* 133

Bites, Mini Hot Dog–Pimiento, *140,* 141

Buffalo Chicken Dip, 42, *43*

Buffalo Chicken Empanadas, 226, *227*

Buffalo Veggie–Stuffed Mushrooms, 154, *155*

Cheddar Cauliflower "Popcorn," *26,* 27

Cheesy Beef and Green Chile Spicy Tacos, *114,* 115

Cherry–Key Lime Pie Pops, *188,* 189

Chocolate-Coconut Marshmallow Dip, 88, *89*

Coconut-Chocolate–Covered Cheesecake Bites, 274, *275*

Cottage, Greek-Style Snack Bowl, *20, 21*

Feta and Spinach–Stuffed Bread, 136, *137*

Flaky Deli Slices, 144, *145*

French Bread Taco Pizza, *138,* 139

Fruit Fish, *64*, 65

Greek Hummus Dip with Dippers, 252, *253*

Grilled Bean Chip Nachos, *130*, 131

Herbed Goat, Pizza Poppers, 120, *121*

Jalapeño–Everything–Seasoned Parmesan Crisps, 14, *15*

Kimchi-Chicken Quesadillas, 112, *113*

Loaded Baked Potato Nachos, 128, *129*

Loaded Chicken Totchos, 134, *135*

Loaded Pizza Scrambled Eggs, 126, *127*

Mediterranean Watermelon "Fries" with Creamy Feta Dip, 24, *25*

Raspberry Cream-Filled Chocolates, *267*, 277

Skinny Fluffy Orange Fruit Dip, 82, *83*

Slow-Cooker Bacon Cheeseburger Dip, *178*, 179

Smoked Salmon Spread, *176*, 177

Snacks, Salsa-Avocado, *16*, 17

Spicy Indian Mozzarella Bites with Curry Aioli, 172, *173*

Spicy Spinach and Artichoke Dip, *168*, 169

Spinach-Feta Naan Pizzas, *230*, 231

Spread, Baked Artichoke and Jalapeño, 48, *49*

Sun-Dried Tomato and Basil Yogurt Bark, *160*, 161

Sun-Dried Tomato and Feta Spread, *36*, 37

Tex-Mex Tailgate Dip, 180, *181*

Cherry(ies)

−Key Lime Pie Pops, *188*, 189

No-Bake Puffed Quinoa and Fruit Bars, 212, *213*

Chicken

and Avocado Mini Taco Boats, 242, *243*

Buffalo, Dip, *42*, 43

Buffalo, Empanadas, 226, *227*

-Kimchi Quesadillas, 112, *113*

Pan-Fried Taco Wings, *238*, 239

Slow-Cooker Bourbon-Honey BBQ Wings, 142, *143*

Taquitos, Oven-Baked Curry, 106, *107*

Tenders, Tennessee Hot Fried, 234, *235*

Totchos, Loaded, 134, *135*

Chiles

Avocado "Jalapeño Popper" Boats, *108*, 109

Baked Artichoke and Jalapeño Cheese Spread, 48, *49*

Blooming Onion with Bacon-Chipotle Dip, 156, *157*

Buffalo Chicken Empanadas, 226, *227*

Green, and Beef Spicy Tacos, Cheesy, *114*, 115

Grilled Bean Chip Nachos, *130*, 131

Jalapeño–Everything–Seasoned Parmesan Crisps, 14, *15*

Loaded Chicken Totchos, 134, *135*

Spiced Pumpkin, Apple and Jalapeño Dip, 194, *195*

Tex-Mex Tailgate Dip, 180, *181*

Chocolate

White,−Drizzled Cereal Mix, *100*, 101

Chocolate(s)

Cinnamon−Waffle Cone Snack Mix, 214, *215*

-Coconut−Covered Cheesecake Bites, 274, *275*

-Coconut Marshmallow Dip, 88, *89*

Dark, Almond Bark Crunchies, 207

Decadent Veggie Brownies, 256, *257*

Double,−Dipped Strawberry Yogurt Cup, *54*, 55

Easy Cracker Toffee, *260*, 261

Energy Balls 3 Ways, *205*, 206

Hot, Winter Mix, 272, *273*

Jack-O'-Lantern Brownies, 258, 259

No-Bake Layered Cinnamon Cereal Bars, 262, *263*

No-Bake Puffed Quinoa and Fruit Bars, 212, *213*

−Peanut Butter Candy Bars, No-Bake, *210*, 211

−Peanut Butter Snack Mix, *218*, 219

Raspberry Cream-Filled, *267*, 277

Salted Caramel Macchiato Brownie Cups, 96, *97*

Sauce, Spicy, Churro Rangoons with, *198*, 199

Strawberry, and Oat "Milk" Shakes, *73*, 75

Turtle Banana Split Yogurt Cups, 58, *59*

Churro Rangoons with Spicy Chocolate Sauce, *198*, 199

Cinnamon−Waffle Cone Snack Mix, 214, *215*

Citrus Crunch Parfait, 68, *69*

Coconut

-Banana Yogurt Cup, *56*, 57

-Berry "Bubble" Parfait, 52, *53*

Caramelized Banana Bowl, *84*, 85

-Chocolate−Covered Cheesecake Bites, 274, *275*

-Chocolate Marshmallow Dip, 88, *89*

Coffee. *See* Cold-Brew

Cold-Brew Yogurt Pops, 70, *71*

Confetti Mug Cake, 78, *79*

Cookie Butter Mug Cakes, 80, *81*

Corn Snack Mix, Spicy Caramel, 98, *99*

Crab Cake Bites, 118, *119*

Cracker Toffee, Easy, *260*, 261

Cranberries

Chewy Oatmeal Snack Bars, *208*, 209

Dark Chocolate Almond Bark Crunchies, 207

Energy Balls 3 Ways, *205*, 206

Cucumbers

Greek-Style Cottage Cheese Snack Bowl, 20, *21*

Tzatziki "Bruschetta," *152*, 153

White Bean Hummus−Filled Vegetables with Gremolata, 174, *175*

Curry Aioli, 172, *173*

Dill, Fresh, Yogurt Dip, 164, *165*

Dipping Sauce

Creamy Wasabi, *158, 159*

Ginger-Soy, *158, 159*

Dips & spreads. *See also* Hummus

Baked Artichoke and Jalapeño Cheese Spread, 48, *49*

Basil-Spinach Dip, 166, *167*

Beer Cheese Dip, *170,* 171

Buffalo Chicken Dip, 42, *43*

Chocolate-Coconut Marshmallow Dip, 88, *89*

Creamy Feta Dip, Mediterranean Watermelon "Fries" with, *24,* 25

Curry Aioli, 172, *173*

Fresh Dill Yogurt Dip, 164, *165*

Grillside Guacamole, 250, *251*

Skinny Fluffy Orange Fruit Dip, 82, *83*

Slow-Cooker Bacon Cheeseburger Dip, *178,* 179

Smoked Salmon Spread, *176,* 177

Southwest Taco Dip, 40, *41*

Spiced Pumpkin, Apple and Jalapeño Dip, 194, *195*

Spicy Spinach and Artichoke Dip, *168,* 169

Strawberry-Marshmallow Fruit Dip, *196,* 197

Sun-Dried Tomato and Feta Spread, *36,* 37

Tex-Mex Tailgate Dip, 180, *181*

Drinks. *See* Oat "Milk"

Edamame, Steamed, in the Shell with Dipping Sauces, *158,* 159

Eggs

Deviled, Parsley, 162, *163*

Scrambled, Loaded Pizza, 126, *127*

Empanadas, Buffalo Chicken, 226, *227*

Empanaditas, Beef, *228,* 229

Energy Balls

3 Ways, *205,* 206

preparing, tips for, 204

Fish. *See* Smoked Salmon

Frozen Banana Pops, 266–67, *266–67*

Fruit. *See also* Berries; *specific fruits*

Dip, Skinny Fluffy Orange, 82, *83*

Dip, Strawberry-Marshmallow, *196,* 197

Fish, *64,* 65

Fruity Yogurt Parfaits, 60, *61*

and Puffed Quinoa Bars, No-Bake, 212, *213*

Fruit-flavored snacks

Fruity Pretzel Crayons, *190,* 191

Ladybug Summertime Fun Snacks, 264, *265*

Masked Turtles Marshmallow Pops, *268,* 269

Ginger-Soy Dipping Sauce, *158,* 159

Gluten-free cooking, 8–10

Graham crackers

Chewy Oatmeal Snack Bars, *208,* 209

Dark Chocolate Almond Bark Crunchies, 207

Granola "Pizzas," Good-for-You, 200, *201*

Greek-Style Cottage Cheese Snack Bowl, 20, *21*

Green Bean "Fries," Spicy, 28, *29*

Guacamole, Grillside, 250, *251*

Ham and prosciutto

Feta and Spinach–Stuffed Bread, 136, *137*

Flaky Deli Slices, 144, *145*

Honey

-Bourbon BBQ Wings, Slow-Cooker, 142, *143*

Chai-Spiced Pan-Fried Bananas, *92,* 93

Hot Dog–Pimiento Cheese Bites, Mini, *140,* 141

Hummus

Dip with Dippers, Greek, 252, *253*

Easy, *33,* 34

Fire-Roasted Tomato, *38,* 39

flavor variations, 32, *32–33*

Olive Spread, 35

Roasted Beet, 248, *249*

and Veggie Cutouts, Fall, 244, *245*

White Bean,–Filled Vegetables with Gremolata, 174, *175*

Italian Carrot "Fries," 30, *31*

Jack-O'-Lantern Brownies, *258,* 259

Jalapeño–Everything–Seasoned Parmesan Crisps, 14, *15*

Kimchi-Chicken Quesadillas, 112, *113*

Ladybug Summertime Fun Snacks, 264, *265*

Lime, Key,–Cherry Pie Pops, *188,* 189

Mango-Banana and Oat "Milk" Smoothies, *73,* 75

Marshmallow creme

Chocolate-Coconut Marshmallow Dip, 88, *89*

No-Bake Layered Cinnamon Cereal Bars, 262, *263*

Strawberry-Marshmallow Fruit Dip, *196*, 197

Marshmallows

Confetti Mug Cake, *78*, 79

Hot Chocolate Winter Mix, 272, *273*

Masked Turtles Marshmallow Pops, *268*, 269

Mini, Peanut Butter–Banana Bites with, 90, *91*

No-Bake Chocolate–Peanut Butter Candy Bars, *210*, 211

No-Bake Layered Cinnamon Cereal Bars, *262*, 263

Raspberry Chocolate Hazelnut Cereal "Nachos," 76

Masked Turtles Marshmallow Pops, *268*, 269

Meatballs, Asian, with Teriyaki Glaze, 232, *233*

Mediterranean Watermelon "Fries" with Creamy Feta Dip, 24, 25

Melon

Kabobs, Mojito, 192, *193*

Mediterranean Watermelon "Fries" with Creamy Feta Dip, *24*, 25

Mojito Melon Kabobs, 192, *193*

Mug Cakes

Confetti, *78*, 79

Cookie Butter, 80, *81*

Mumbai Crisps, *150*, 151

Mushrooms

Buffalo Veggie–Stuffed, 154, *155*

Chick Pea and Veggie Burgers, *116*, 117

Nachos

Beer Queso, *132*, 133

Grilled Bean Chip, *130*, 131

Loaded Baked Potato, 128, *129*

"Nachos"

Pear, *62*, 63

Raspberry Chocolate Hazelnut Cereal, 76

Nut(s). *See also* Almond(s); Peanuts

No-Bake Layered Cinnamon Cereal Bars, 262, *263*

Slow-Cooker Caramel Corn, *270*, 271

Spicy Roasted, Trail Mix, *44*, 45

Sugared Rosemary Snack Mix, 222, *223*

Toasted Rosemary, 182, *183*

Oat "Milk"

10-Minute, *73*, 74

Chai Latte, Iced, *72*, 74

Chocolate, and Strawberry Shakes, *73*, 75

making your own, 72

and Mango-Banana Smoothies, *73*, 75

Oats. *See also* Oat "Milk"

Chewy Oatmeal Snack Bars, *208*, 209

Energy Balls 3 Ways, *205*, 206

Olive(s)

Beef Empanaditas, *228*, 229

Hummus Spread, 35

Tex-Mex Tailgate Dip, 180, *181*

Warm Lemon Rosemary, 149

Onion, Blooming, with Bacon-Chipotle Dip, 156, *157*

Orange Fruit Dip, Skinny Fluffy, 82, *83*

Parfaits

Blueberry Crunch, *86*, 87

Citrus Crunch, 68, *69*

Coconut-Berry "Bubble," 52, *53*

Fruity Yogurt, 60, *61*

Parsley Deviled Eggs, 162, *163*

Pasta

Bacon Mac and Cheese Bowl, 22, *23*

Oven-Toasted Ravioli, *122*, 123

Peach "Cobbler" Snack, Quick, *94*, 95

Peanut Butter

–Banana Bites with Mini Marshmallows, 90, *91*

–Chocolate Candy Bars, No-Bake, *210*, 211

–Chocolate Snack Mix, *218*, 219

Energy Balls 3 Ways, *205*, 206

Peanuts

Chocolate–Peanut Butter Snack Mix, *218*, 219

No-Bake Chocolate–Peanut Butter Candy Bars, *210*, 211

Ultimate Tailgate Party Mix, *46*, 47

Pear "Nachos," *62*, 63

Pepperoni

Flaky Deli Slices, 144, *145*

Loaded Pizza Scrambled Eggs, 126, *127*

Peppers. *See also* Chiles

Fall Hummus and Veggie Cutouts, 244, *245*

French Bread Taco Pizza, *138*, 139

Herbed Goat Cheese Pizza Poppers, 120, *121*

Loaded Pizza Scrambled Eggs, 126, *127*

Mumbai Crisps, *150*, 151

White Bean Hummus–Filled Vegetables with Gremolata, 174, *175*

Pizzas

French Bread Taco, *138*, 139

Spinach-Feta Naan, *230*, 231

"Pizzas," Granola, Good-for-You, 200, *201*

Popcorn

Birthday Cake, *216*, 217

Celebration Snack Mix, *102*, 103

Slow-Cooker Caramel Corn, 270, 271

Ultimate Tailgate Party Mix, *46*, 47

"Popcorn," Cheddar Cauliflower, *26*, 27

Pops

Cherry–Key Lime Pie, *188*, 189

Cold-Brew Yogurt, *70*, 71

Frozen Banana, 266–67, *266–67*

Masked Turtles Marshmallow, *268*, 269

Pork. *See also* Bacon; Pepperoni
    Feta and Spinach–Stuffed Bread, 136, *137*
    Flaky Deli Slices, 144, *145*
    Loaded Pizza Scrambled Eggs, 126, *127*
    Mini Hot Dog–Pimiento Cheese Bites, 140, *141*
Potato(es)
    Baked, Loaded, Nachos, 128, *129*
    Loaded Chicken Totchos, 134, *135*
    Mumbai Crisps, *150*, 151
Potato nugget hacks, 236
Pretzel(s)
    Crayons, Fruity, *190*, 191
    Slow-Cooker Caramel Corn, *270*, 271
    Spicy Caramel Corn Snack Mix, 98, *99*
    Spicy Roasted Nut Trail Mix, 44, *45*
    Sugared Rosemary Snack Mix, 222, *223*
    Ultimate Tailgate Party Mix, *46*, 47
Pumpkin, Spiced, Apple, and Jalapeño Dip, 194, *195*

Quesadillas, Kimchi-Chicken, 112, *113*
Quinoa, Puffed, and Fruit Bars, No-Bake, 212, *213*

Rainbow Shebang Snack Mix, 220, *221*
Raspberry
    Chocolate Hazelnut Cereal "Nachos," 76
    Cream-Filled Chocolates, *267*, 277
    Streusel Snack Cake, 202, *203*
Ravioli, Oven-Toasted, *122*, 123
Rosemary
    Nuts, Toasted, 182, *183*
    Snack Mix, Sugared, 222, *223*

Salsa-Avocado Cheese Snacks, *16*, 17
Salted Caramel Macchiato Brownie Cups, 96, *97*
Sausages
    Mini Hot Dog–Pimiento Cheese Bites, 140, *141*
Seafood
    Crab Cake Bites, 118, *119*
    Smoked Salmon Spread, *176*, 177
Shakes, Chocolate, Strawberry and Oat "Milk," *73*, 75
Smoked Salmon Spread, *176*, 177
Smoothies, Mango-Banana and Oat "Milk," *73*, 75
Snack Mixes
    Celebration, *102*, 103
    Chocolate–Peanut Butter, *218*, 219
    Cinnamon–Waffle Cone, *214*, 215
    Corn, Spicy Caramel, 98, *99*
    Hot Chocolate Winter Mix, 272, *273*
    Rainbow Shebang, 220, *221*
    Sugared Rosemary, 222, *223*
    Ultimate Tailgate Party Mix, *46*, 47
    White Chocolate-Drizzled Cereal Mix, *100*, 101
Southwest Taco Dip, 40, *41*
Soy-Ginger Dipping Sauce, *158*, 159
Spinach
    and Artichoke Dip, Spicy, *168*, 169
    -Basil Dip, 166, *167*
    -Feta Naan Pizzas, *230*, 231
    and Feta–Stuffed Bread, 136, *137*
Strawberry(ies)
    Chocolate, and Oat "Milk" Shakes, *73*, 75
    Coconut-Berry "Bubble" Parfait, 52, *53*
    Fruity Yogurt Parfaits, 60, *61*
    -Lemon Shortcake Bowl, 66, *67*
    -Marshmallow Fruit Dip, *196*, 197
    Yogurt Cup, Double Chocolate–Dipped, *54*, 55

Taco Boats, Mini, Chicken and Avocado, 242, *243*
Tacos
    Beefy Bacon Ranch Spicy, *240*, 241
    Spicy, Cheesy Beef and Green Chile, *114*, 115
Taquitos, Oven-Baked Curry Chicken, 106, *107*
Tex-Mex Tailgate Dip, 180, *181*
Toffee, Easy Cracker, *260*, 261
Tomato(es)
    Fire-Roasted, Hummus, *38*, 39
    Greek-Style Cottage Cheese Snack Bowl, 20, *21*
    Grilled Bean Chip Nachos, *130*, 131
    Grillside Guacamole, 250, *251*
    Loaded Chicken Totchos, 134, *135*
    Savory Caprese Bowl, *18*, 19
    Southwest Taco Dip, 40, *41*
    Sun-Dried, and Basil Yogurt Bark, *160*, 161
    Sun-Dried, and Feta Spread, *36*, 37
    Tex-Mex Tailgate Dip, 180, *181*
    White Bean Hummus–Filled Vegetables with Gremolata, 174, *175*
Tortilla chips
    Beer Queso Nachos, *132*, 133
    Mumbai Crisps, *150*, 151
    Tzatziki "Bruschetta," *152*, 153
Tortillas
    Avocado "Jalapeño Popper" Boats, *108*, 109
    Bacon Jalapeño Turkey Roll-Ups, *110*, 111
    Cheesy Beef and Green Chile Spicy Tacos, *114*, 115
    Chicken and Avocado Mini Taco Boats, 242, *243*
    Kimchi-Chicken Quesadillas, 112, *113*
    Oven-Baked Curry Chicken Taquitos, 106, *107*
Trail Mix, Spicy Roasted Nut, 44, *45*

Turkey Jalapeño Bacon Roll-Ups, *110,* 111

Turtle Banana Split Yogurt Cups, 58, *59*

Tzatziki "Bruschetta," *152,* 153

Vegan diets, 11

Vegetables. *See also specific vegetables*

Buffalo Veggie–Stuffed Mushrooms, 154, *155*

Chick Pea and Veggie Burgers, *116,* 117

Fall Hummus and Veggie Cutouts, 244, *245*

Vegetarian diets, 11

Waffle Cone–Cinnamon Snack Mix, 214, *215*

Wasabi Dipping Sauce, Creamy, *158,* 159

Watermelon "Fries," Mediterranean, with Creamy Feta Dip, *24,* 25

White Chocolate–Drizzled Cereal Mix, *100,* 101

Yogurt

Bark, Sun-Dried Tomato and Basil, *160,* 161

Basil-Spinach Dip, 166, *167*

Blueberry Crunch Parfait, *86,* 87

Caramelized Banana Bowl, *84,* 85

Citrus Crunch Parfait, 68, *69*

Coconut-Berry "Bubble" Parfait, 52, *53*

Cup, Banana-Coconut, *56,* 57

Cup, Double Chocolate–Dipped Strawberry, *54,* 55

Cups, Turtle Banana Split, 58, *59*

Galactic Fro-Yo Bark, 186, *187*

Good-for-You Granola "Pizzas," 200, *201*

Greek Hummus Dip with Dippers, 252, *253*

Mediterranean Watermelon "Fries" with Creamy Feta Dip, *24,* 25

Parfaits, Fruity, 60, *61*

-Parmesan Dip, Baked Zucchini Sticks with, *246,* 247

Pops, Cold-Brew, *70,* 71

Quick Peach "Cobbler" Snack, *94,* 95

Savory Caprese Bowl, *18,* 19

Skinny Fluffy Orange Fruit Dip, 82, *83*

Southwest Taco Dip, 40, *41*

Strawberry-Lemon Shortcake Bowl, 66, *67*

Strawberry-Marshmallow Fruit Dip, *196,* 197

Sun-Dried Tomato and Feta Spread, *36,* 37

Tzatziki "Bruschetta," *152,* 153

Zucchini

Buffalo Veggie–Stuffed Mushrooms, 154, *155*

Fall Hummus and Veggie Cutouts, 244, *245*

Sticks, Baked, with Parmesan-Yogurt Dip, *246,* 247

Hungry for more?

Don't miss these other great Betty Crocker cookbooks

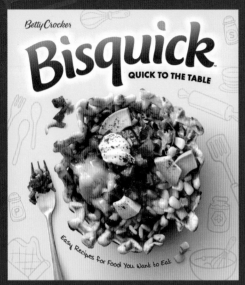

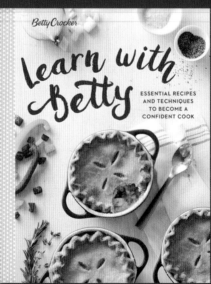